Going Comprehensive

LIBRARY OF POLITICAL STUDIES

GENERAL EDITOR:

PROFESSOR H. VICTOR WISEMAN
Department of Government
University of Exeter

Going Comprehensive

Educational policy-making in two county boroughs

by Richard Batley
formerly Research Assistant, Tyneside Research Project

Oswald O'Brien
Staff Tutor in Industrial Studies, University of Durham

Henry Parris
Professor in Politics, University of Waterloo, Ontario
(formerly Director, Tyneside Research Project)

LONDON
ROUTLEDGE & KEGAN PAUL

First published 1970
by Routledge & Kegan Paul Ltd
Broadway House, 68-74 Carter Lane
London, E.C.4
Printed in Great Britain
by Northumberland Press Ltd
Gateshead
© Richard Batley, Oswald O'Brien and Henry Parris 1970
ISBN 0 7100 6838 7

Contents

CONTENTS

General editor's introduction

This series of monographs is designed primarily to meet the needs of students of government, politics, or political science in Universities and other institutions providing courses leading to degrees. Each volume aims to provide a brief general introduction indicating the significance of its topic, e.g., executives, parties, pressure groups, etc., and then a longer 'case study' relevant to the general topic. First-year students will thus be introduced to the kind of detailed work on which all generalizations must be based, while more mature students will have an opportunity to become acquainted with recent original research in a variety of fields. The series will eventually provide a comprehensive coverage of most aspects of political science in a more interesting and fundamental manner than in the large volume which often fails to compensate in breadth for what it inevitably lacks in depth.

The politics of education—especially of comprehensive schools, are much in the public eye at present. There are differences between and within parties. Relations between central and local government are involved. The 'customer', parent or pupil, sometimes appears to be more active than in other fields of public policy. Local authorities adopt different attitudes; sometimes Labour-controlled councils are reluctant to 'go comprehensive'; sometimes Conservative-controlled councils are proud of their 'progressive' policies. Having provided an informative general introduction to the problem, the authors of this monograph examine in detail the adoption of comprehensive schemes in two very similar county boroughs. We see at work central and local government, pressure groups, the Press, public opinion. Political and social ideas, the decision-making process, the influence of groups and individuals, are all revealed. Students of politics and public administration should find this a fascinating exercise. But the book should appeal also to those primarily interested in education and, indeed, to a wider general public. It is a valuable addition to the Library of Political Studies.

H.V.W.

(Professor Wiseman had written this Introduction before his death in November 1969.)

Acknowledgements

We acknowledge with thanks the help of the Social Science Research Council who financed the Gateshead section of this study. We are also indebted to all those who talked to us, or gave access to information not otherwise available. Without their co-operation it would have been impossible to write this book. In particular, we should mention Mr D. Peter, Chief Education Officer of Darlington, Mr F. A. Stokes, Director of Education for Gateshead, and Dr Margherita Rendel. Besides assisting us in other ways, they have read the book in typescript and we have benefited from their comments. We alone remain, however, responsible for any defects still to be found in these pages.

Richard Batley
Oswald O'Brien
Henry Parris

1

Introduction

In Liverpool, in 1964,

> nearly fifteen hundred secondary schoolchildren spent part of their holiday in demonstrating for and against comprehensive education. The largest demonstration was by a thousand grammar schoolchildren who marched through the city centre to hand in at the education offices a petition opposing the local authority's decision to introduce a comprehensive scheme next September. An hour later, nearly three hundred pupils from the Croxteth Secondary Modern Girls' School, joined by a few other girls from other schools, marched on the offices and handed in a petition in favour of a comprehensive scheme, with a letter of good wishes for its success. These girls sang slogans to modern tunes as they marched, but were told by the police not to ring a big brass hand-bell they carried—the bell, they said, which was tolled by Lord Hailsham at a Conservative conference a few years ago.

A few weeks later, the Secretary of State had received some 400 individual letters of objection to the Liverpool scheme (*Times Educational Supplement*, 30 October and 20 November, 1964).

Liverpool was not the only place where feelings ran high on the comprehensive issue. 'Clinging in the rain to their hoisted standards, the sodden parents from Bristol marched' through London one Saturday afternoon in December 1964.

> They advanced slowly, from Speakers' Corner to Trafalgar Square, like a Roman phalanx, their umbrellas massed in the traditional *testudo*. They were protesting against the Bristol comprehensive plan. 'No dictatorship—choice for parents', the banners read; 'Goodbye parents' freedom'; 'Wilson pre-election pledge: "Grammar Schools will be abolished over my dead body"— And now?' ... Bristol's protest—Freedom in Education ... [was the slogan of the Bristol parents, more than a hundred of them] and they were followed in their solemn progress by parents and children from all over the country.

This was the second demonstration in London. A little earlier, Bristolians had marched on the Department of Education and Science, and on 10 Downing Street, to deliver letters of protest. Far larger numbers had, naturally enough, been involved in Bristol itself. During the six-hour debate which led to the adoption of the comprehensive plan by the city council, and while the Opposition accused the Labour majority of ignoring petitions signed by 28,000 people, 'opponents of the plan paraded outside the council buildings. Banners carried by demonstrators bore the words "Hands off our grammar schools" and "Bristol has a fine system of education—why change it?" ' (*Times Educational Supplement*, 16 October, 13 November, and 11 December, 1964).

From these and other cases, it appears that the comprehensive schools issue is one that rouses deep concern and brings out into the streets people who normally show little interest in public life. As part of a study of participation in government in north-east England, therefore, it seemed worth while to look at the process of going comprehensive in two education authorities in order to see who took part, and how exactly the decision came to be taken. Before going into the field, however, it is necessary to summarize the development of the comprehensive schools movement in this country.

The comprehensive schools movement

The 1944 Act required local education authorities to provide secondary education for all, but left them to decide what form it should take. However, a circular of December 1945, issued by the Ministry of Education to guide local authorities in the development of secondary schools, proceeded on the assumption that a tripartite pattern of grammar, technical and modern schools would normally prevail. Such a pattern was in line with current psychological thought. For a generation, educational psychologists had been primarily concerned with mental measurement. As long ago as 1926, the Hadow Committee had been assured that it was possible by means of intelligence tests to make a fairly accurate assessment of a child's mental capacity by the age of twelve. If this were so, it would be feasible to make the break between the primary and secondary stages at eleven-plus, and to provide three different types of secondary schools for three different levels of intellectual ability. The Spens Committee in 1938 specifically recommended that secondary education should develop along these lines, and the influence of the doctrine was clearly to be seen in the White Paper which paved the way for the 1944 Act. At this stage, there was nothing partisan about such a policy. The 1944 Act was carried by a Coalition Government. The 1945 circular was issued on the authority of a Labour minister. Tripartite secondary education was acceptable to most Conservatives since it reflected a hierarchical view of society. It was also acceptable to the majority of the Labour Party because it extended the opportunity of secondary educa-

3

tion, previously the privilege of a minority, to everyone.

However, from an early date, dissentient voices were raised. In sparsely populated rural areas, the tripartite system was cumbersome and unwieldy. Either the new schools would have to remain small, with consequent drawbacks in staffing and equipment, or else the catchment areas would have to be large, which would impose a high cost—in both human and economic terms—in travelling. The pragmatic solution was to have a single secondary school for all the children in an area. Anglesey is probably the best example of a local education authority which has adopted this solution. It has four such schools. The first, Holyhead, was founded in 1949 by the merger of a grammar and a modern school. Others followed at Almwch, Beaumaris and Llangefni. Incidentally, all are co-educational, since the arguments against separate schools for different levels of ability in such an area also apply to separate provision for girls and boys.

Elsewhere, tripartitism called forth criticisms which had wider implications. The West Riding's Educational Development Plan (1948) declared:

> the committee ... have been unable to accept certain suggestions which have been made or implied in various reports or ministerial circulars. They cannot, for instance, agree that at the age of eleven children can be classified into three recognized mental types, and should be allocated to grammar, modern, and technical schools accordingly ... [or] that at the age of eleven children show certain aptitudes which can be relied upon to indicate the type of secondary school to which a child should be allocated.

Such a statement implies a philosophy of society. In this context, comprehensive education could become, quite properly, a political issue. Conservatives could legitimately object because of its egalitarian implications. Socialists could incorporate the comprehensive school into their

4

ideology, seeing it as a potent instrument of social change.

Such was the background, in particular, of the comprehensive schools programme in London. The Labour majority on the London County Council looked to education, in the words of the London School Plan (1947), to 'promote a feeling of social unity among adolescents of all kinds and degrees of ability'. Their policy led to conflict with Conservative Ministers of Education from 1951 onwards. Although a local education authority could develop a new secondary school as a comprehensive, the Minister's permission was needed to close an existing one or change its status. Yet if established selective schools continue to exist in the same catchment areas as new comprehensive schools, there is a real danger that the inferiority of the latter would prove to be a self-fulfilling prophecy. The former would, in all probability, go on attracting the best talent, both among staff and among pupils. Hence, the new system would never get a fair chance to show what it could do. When, therefore, the L.C.C. built its first large new comprehensive, Kidbrooke, it proposed to close Eltham Hill Girls' Grammar School and transfer the pupils to the new establishment. The Minister in 1954 refused permission. Neither would she allow the L.C.C. to expand Bec Boys' Grammar School into a comprehensive. In spite of such obstacles, by 1965 45 per cent of the London secondary school population was housed in new comprehensive schools.

Assuming the desirability of comprehensive education, the most obvious way to provide it is to put up a new building capable of taking the required number of children from eleven to eighteen. Given the restrictions on school building, such a course is often not possible. Other patterns have been worked out, two of which call for notice here. The first of these is the Leicestershire Plan, so called from the county which pioneered it. The main feature of it is that it transforms the secondary modern schools in a neighbourhood from negatively selective schools fed by children who have 'failed' the eleven-plus to Junior High Schools taking all children up to the age of fourteen. Those whose parents undertake to keep them at school for at least two more years may then transfer to a Senior High School (the former grammar school). When the school-leaving age is raised to 16, all children will go on for at least two years to the Senior High School. The Leicestershire Plan, with modifications where required, has been widely adopted by other authorities.

The other approach of special interest here is the sixth form college, pioneered by Croydon. In this scheme, all secondary schools retain children to the age of 16 only. Those who wish to stay longer at school move to a separate institution for their sixth form work. Unlike the Leicestershire Plan, it strikes at what has come to be regarded as the essence of the grammar school by cutting off its advanced work. For this reason, grammar school teachers and their supporters have vigorously opposed it. Another objection is that a good many children may not go on to a sixth form college because the change from school to college would coincide with the school-leaving age, once it has been raised to 16. On the other hand, it may well be in keeping with the needs of older pupils, many of whom now feel that they should be regarded as students rather than as schoolchildren.

Successive Conservative ministers between 1951 and 1964 at no time put a complete stop to the development of comprehensive education by local education authorities. The White Paper of December 1958 recognized the value of 'experiments' with comprehensive schools, so long as they were 'proposed on genuine educational grounds'. Such experiments would be especially welcome in sparsely populated country districts, and in extensive new housing districts lacking schools with a 'well-established tradition'. Nevertheless, the return of Labour to power in 1964 has an obvious importance in the story. At that time, although only about one child in fourteen

6

was in a comprehensive, the trend seemed to be clear:

> The division of the secondary school population into categories at the age of 11 [had] become increasingly intolerable in a society in which gross social inequalities are no longer acceptable. Selective schools can only count on unqualified public support when class divisions are firm and unchallenged. Once the demand for, if not the actuality of, social equality has reached a certain point, pressures develop to bring a non-differentiated pattern of schooling over at least the first part of the secondary stage. ... A stage ... has been reached in England ... when an increasing number of parents challenge and reject the relegation of their children to schools ... which mark them as inferior to their fellows (Baron, 112).

There were others prepared to fight a rear-guard action:

> Change in the direction of the ... comprehensive school is, however, a matter of bitter contention. It disturbs middle-class parents, who feel that it matters intensely that their children should be educated among those of similar family background (Baron, 112-3).

The Minister's powers

Had the protesting Liverpudlians and Bristolians succeeded in winning over the Secretary of State, what in fact could he have done? The 1944 Education Act appears to give the Minister very extensive power over a local authority. It begins:

> It shall be lawful for His Majesty to appoint a Minister ... whose duty it shall be to promote the education of the people of England and Wales and the progressive development of institutions devoted to that purpose, and to secure the effective execution by local authorities, under his control and direction, of the national policy for providing a varied and comprehensive educational service in every area.

Another provision (s.68) is even more strongly worded. It reads: 'If the Minister is satisfied ... that any local education authority ... have acted or are proposing to act unreasonably' with respect to the exercise of any power or the performance of any duty imposed by the Act, he may give directions accordingly. On the other hand, the Act says nothing about the kinds of schools in which secondary education is to be provided. Hence, when the Department of Education and Science wishes to influence the pattern of secondary education in a local authority, it has to use powers not intended primarily, if at all, for that purpose.

The Act requires a local education authority to obtain the approval of the Department for the establishment of a new school. S.13 lays down that where a local authority intends to set up a new school it shall put proposals for that purpose before the Secretary of State; that the latter may approve such proposals after making such modifications, if any, as appear desirable; that an authority shall not, without the leave of the Secretary of State, do anything covered by the s.13 procedure until the Secretary of State's approval has been obtained. There have been cases where approval has been withheld not because the Minister disputed the need for a new secondary school, but because he did not favour the type of secondary school proposed:

> During the last few years, for educational, political, and social reasons, many local authorities have resolved to introduce many different patterns of secondary education. And the Department, becoming alarmed by the diversity of these patterns and, in some cases, by the details of the proposed changes, has sought to influence local authorities more generally. But because of the omissions in the Act of 1944, the powers of the Department have been limited.... The absence of statutory provisions to enable the Department to control the patterns of secondary education is anomalous, and ...

8

the working relationship between the Department and the local authorities has been much affected by these omissions (Griffith, 51).

The limits of the Department's power were shown in the negotiations which led to the issue of Circular 10/65 on comprehensive reorganization. The opposition to comprehensive schools was strong and not confined to the Conservative ranks; many Labour L.E.A.s made no move to reorganize. From 1960, however, more and more authorities sought to change to the comprehensive system. For some time before they went out of office in 1964 the Conservative Government had ceased blocking schemes for reorganization. There did seem to be a need for the Minister to give a clear statement of national policy. In the circular, the Secretary of State requested 'local education authorities, if they have not already done so, to prepare and submit to him plans for reorganizing secondary education in their areas on comprehensive lines. The purpose of this circular is to provide some central guidance on the methods by which this can be achieved.' Six main forms of comprehensive education were set out and discussed. The views of the D.E.S. on buildings, staffing and ages of transfer were given. L.E.A.s were told that the plans should, after consultation with the churches, include voluntary schools. The views of those who work the system should also be taken into account:

> The proper processes of local government must leave initiative on matters of principle and the ultimate responsibility for decisions with the elected representatives of the community. But the Secretary of State believes that once the principles and main outlines of a possible plan of reorganization have been formulated there should follow a period of close and genuine consultation with teachers.

What legal force had Circular 10/65? Bournemouth

informed the Secretary of State that the changes called for were, in its case, 'unnecessary and undesirable'. In such a situation, it is hard to see any statutory power which would enable the Secretary of State to carry out his policy. From his point of view, would not a new Educational Act have been preferable? Nevertheless, the power of a circular should not be underrated. As an anonymous legal correspondent pointed out a year after it came out, no one had challenged the validity of 10/65. There was

> ... little hope of doing so successfully. The 1944 Education Act conferred upon the minister a duty ... 'to secure the effective execution' of 'the national policy' for education. The minister is thus entitled ... to cajole the local education authorities into executing the 'national policy'. And local education authorities are obliged to act in such matters 'under his control and direction'. This is not a power to coerce ... (*Times Educational Supplement*, 1 July, 1966).

But it is a substantial power to persuade. The Minister's influence in practice goes further because he can, under s.13, refuse approval of new building. He has, in fact, threatened to use this power to refuse new building to local education authorities which do not produce satisfactory comprehensive schemes.

Any legal challenge to the circular would have to rely on the words 'a varied and comprehensive educational service in every area'. (The use of the word 'comprehensive' in two senses introduces an unfortunate complication.) It could be argued that a local education authority with only one type of secondary school (i.e., comprehensives) would be failing in its duty to comply with this provision, which occurs in s.1 of the Act. If this were held to be so, the Secretary of State could hardly have the power to urge local education authorities by circular to break the law. An objector would go on to cite s.8, which states that a local authority's schools must be

sufficient in number, character and equipment to afford
for all pupils opportunities for education offering such
a variety of instruction and training as may be desirable
in view of their different ages, abilities and aptitudes
and of the differing periods for which they may be
expected to remain at school including practical instruction and training appropriate to their respective needs.

There does not seem to be much in this. Any champion of
comprehensive education would argue that varied provision of the kind indicated can be made available within
each comprehensive school as well as, if not better than,
within the separate schools of the tripartite system.

Two leading cases: Ealing and Enfield

Such are the Minister's powers. But after 10/65, there
was clearly no chance of persuading him to use them to
hold back the development of comprehensives. So parents
who wished to do so turned to the courts instead. The
law appeared to promise protection. *Wood v. Ealing
Borough Council*, a case decided in 1966, put the question
to the test. The action was brought on behalf of the Joint
Parents Committee of Grammar Schools of Ealing, which
claimed the support of 10,000 parents. An injunction was
sought to restrain the authority from reorganizing certain
schools on comprehensive lines. A number of issues were
raised by the parents and decided by the judge. From
the present point of view, the most important was the
interpretation of s.76 of the Education Act, 1944, which
lays down that 'in the exercise and performance of all
powers and duties conferred and imposed on them by
this Act ... local education authorities shall have regard
to the general principle that ... pupils are to be educated
in accordance with the wishes of their parents'. To the
lay mind, this appears to mean that, before reorganizing
its schools, a local education authority should find out
what kind of schools parents desire. It is true that 'parents

had been invited to meetings at which local officials explained the proposals, but ... parents had been limited to one question each and had not been given an opportunity to express their views'. Mr Justice Goff admitted that this was not consultation: '... on the evidence it is clear that the parents were presented with a *fait accompli* ... their views were ... reported to the working committee ... [only] after the adoption of the scheme. The parents were in no sense consulted' (*Times Educational Supplement*, 29 July, 1966).

Nevertheless, the judge ruled that there had been no breach of s.76 which 'meant no more than that the local education authority had to take into account the general principle, weighing it in the balance with other considerations'. He accepted the contention of defence counsel that the local authority had to consider the wishes of particular parents in respect of their own particular children but not the wishes of parents generally:

> I think it would be wholly impracticable if the Act meant that the wishes of parents in general had to be considered, since they would ... not agree in most, if not all, cases, and would, moreover, be a constantly fluctuating body. ... In essence I felt throughout that the parents were in this difficulty: that, though their counsel disclaimed this, they were in reality trying to establish a general right to be consulted as to the revision of the development plan ... and I still feel that is the real nature of their case. I can find no support for it in the Act, which, in fact, appears to negative it.

The basic aim of the plaintiffs in *Bradbury & others* v. *London Borough of Enfield* was similar to that of the Ealing parents. But of course they had to rest their case on different arguments. At Enfield there had been discussions about going comprehensive with a teachers' consultative committee which 'split into five working parties and each was asked to list advantages, disadvantages, and the suitability for Enfield of the schemes listed in Circular

10/65'. The disadvantages only were extracted from the report of the working parties and circulated in an anonymous document headed 'The Other Side of the Comprehensive Story: Please Read & Pass to Another Parent'. It was signed 'The Vigilantes' (*Times Educational Supplement*, 1 July, 1966). An Enfield Joint Parents' Emergency Committee was formed, which collected 10,000 signatures to a petition (*Times Educational Supplement*, 25 November, 1966).

Eventually an injunction was sought to restrain the authority from introducing a comprehensive scheme which had already been approved by the Minister. The main ground alleged was that the change in character of certain selective schools was so great as to constitute closure, followed by the opening of a new school on the same premises. Before closing a school, a local education authority has to comply with the procedure laid down in s.13 of the 1944 Act. This had not been done, and the authority had been told it was not necessary. In the words of the Master of the Rolls, 'the council said that they were advised by the minister that no such notices were required. But the advice of the minister was not law'. The parents got their injunction (on appeal) pending compliance with the s.13 procedure.

> After all, the Department of Education and the local education authorities were subject to the rule of law and must comply with it.... Although there might be considerable upset for a number of people, it was far more important that an education authority and the Department should observe the law and the requirements which Parliament had expressly laid down to see that people's views were heard and that the electors could make their objections heard and have them properly considered. The injunction should therefore go to see that the authority kept to the law (*Times Educational Supplement*, 25 August, 1967).

That was not the end of the Enfield story, but this is

not the place to tell the whole of it. The point that should
be made is that a legal struggle between citizens and a
Minister is never equal, because it is always open to the
Minister to change the law. That is what happened in
this instance. The Secretary of State promoted a new
Education Bill. As a result, the parents concluded that
further legal action would be hopeless (*Times Educational
Supplement*, 15 December, 1967). Hence, the main issue—
whether the reorganization was *ultra vires* or not—never
came to trial. Even had it done so, and the verdict gone
in favour of the parents, the ultimate outcome would not
necessarily have been very different, because the Minister
could still have gone back to Parliament for new powers.
An education officer, writing anonymously, had already
pointed out the limited scope of legal remedies in a situation of this kind:

> The court was not concerned with the fundamental
> rights of local citizens, nor with the virtues or follies of
> educational reorganization on a comprehensive pattern,
> but with the much more mundane issues of compliance
> with s.13 of the Education Act, 1944, with the meaning
> of the word 'maintain', and with what precisely con-
> stitutes a change in the fundamental character of ... a
> school. It decided that change in age range or in the
> sex group for which a school caters are fundamental
> and necessitate compliance with s.13, while an
> alteration in the curriculum, based on comprehensive
> principles, is not.... Pronouncements based on legal
> technicalities should never be construed as victories on
> major educational policy (*Times Educational Supple-
> ment*, 1 September, 1967).

Darlington and Gateshead: the background to politics

The alternative to legal action had already been indicated
by defence counsel in the Ealing case:

> This was really a political issue, the proper remedy for

which was through the ballot box and not through the law. What the plaintiffs ... were really complaining about was that, first of all, they did not like the national policy of comprehensive education. The second thing they complained of in particular was the method by which the Ealing education authority proposed to implement that policy. Those were both matters which should be remedied, not by the court, but by the ballot box in government or local government elections (*Times Educational Supplement*, 29 July, 1966).

The question was settled by political means both in Darlington and Gateshead. What factors—historical, economic and social—condition political behaviour in those towns?

	DARLINGTON		GATESHEAD		National
	Value	Rank	Value	Rank	Median
1951 Population ('000)					
% aged 0-14	22·2	67	24·4	26	21·8
% aged 15-64	66·9	94	66·4	114	67·3
% aged 65 or over	10·9	68	9·2	121	10·4
Population change					
1931-51—total (%)	17·8	61	− 7·6	141	11·0
1931-51—due to births & deaths	8·5	86	10·3	69	9·0
1931-51—due to other causes	9·3	65	−17·9	147	2·5
1951-8	− 2·0	106	− 4·5	139	− 0·2
1950-2 birth rate as % of national rate	97	74	115	17	96
1955-7 birth rate as % of national rate	96	74	108	25	94
Households & housing					
% h/holds of six or more persons	8·3	52	10·9	13	7·2
% 1-3 room dwellings	19·9	22	50·1	1	10·6
Persons per room	0·79	22	0·97	1	0·74
% overcrowded households (composite)	8·1	36	20·9	1	5·9
% households at over 1½ persons per room	6·2	35	16·5	1	4·3

| | DARLINGTON | | GATESHEAD | | National |
	Value	Rank	Value	Rank	Median
% h/holds with piped water	95	52	85	148	94·0
% h/holds with piped water, W.C., cooking stove, kitchen sink, fixed bath	68	71	45	147	65·0
Houses built 1945-58 per 1,000 pop. in 1951	44	91	40	100	48
Local authority houses built 1945-58 per 1,000 pop. in 1951	32	80	38	61	32
% of houses built 1945-58 by local authorities	73·5	74	94·0	5	72·8

(*Source*: C. A. Moser & W. Scott, *British Towns*, 1961.)

Superficially, Darlington and Gateshead appear to be much alike. They are similar in size and only thirty miles or so apart from each other. Both are industrial in character. Nevertheless there are many differences, some of which seem to throw light on the development of their respective educational policies. In the 1950s, when the story begins, the population of Darlington was rising, whereas that of Gateshead was falling. Between 1931 and 1951, Darlington increased by 17·8 per cent, of which 8·5 per cent was due to an excess of births over deaths, and 9·3 per cent to other causes. During the same period, Gateshead declined. If births and deaths had been the only factors at work, there would have been a rise of 10·3 per cent. In fact, other causes took away 17·9 per cent of the population, with the result that there was a net loss of 7·6 per cent. During the period 1951-8, there was a downward trend in Darlington also, which lost 2·0 per cent of its population. But meanwhile, Gateshead was falling even faster, losing 4·5 per cent of its people during the same seven years. Yet at the same time, the birth-rate in Gateshead was well above the national average, whereas in Darlington, it was slightly below. The picture of Gateshead which emerges is that of a town with a higher than average number of children to educate in each generation, many of whom are soon lost to the town by migration. In Darlington, on the other hand, the pressure on the schools seems to have been much closer to the national norm. In 1951, the proportion of its population in the 0-14 age group was exactly the same as the median for forty-nine northern towns with populations of 50,000 or over (Moser & Scott, 44).

The second point to stress is that Darlington was a more prosperous town than Gateshead during the period covered by this book. The indicator that shows this most strikingly, perhaps, is *per capita* retail sales. The figure for Darlington—£159—was nearly twice as high as that for Gateshead—£88—against a national median of £125. Rateable values tell the same story: over £16 per head for Darlington as against less than £12 for Gateshead. (These figures date from 1961.) By most of Moser & Scott's housing indicators, Darlington was a little below the national median, but not much. By comparison with their median figures for 49 northern towns (Moser & Scott, 44), the gap is even less. In one important respect, Darlington was much better off than most northern towns. 68 per cent of its households had the five standard amenities (piped water, W.C., cooking stove, kitchen sink and fixed bath) as compared with a median of 59 per cent. Gateshead, on the other hand, was among the worst housed towns in the country. In four respects it was worse off than any other of the 157 towns in Moser & Scott's study. It had the highest number of one-to-three-room dwellings, of persons per room, of over-crowded households, and of households with more than 1·5 persons per room. On the other hand, only 85 per cent of its households had piped water, and only 45 per cent had the five standard amenities—well below the median, and

17

near the bottom of the table of all towns in the sample.

This background should be borne in mind in considering how the two towns tackled their educational problems. In 1951, 72·9 per cent of Darlington's population had completed their full-time education before they were fifteen—a proportion exactly equal to the northern median (Moser & Scott, 45) though a little higher than the national median. The corresponding figure for Gateshead was 82·4 per cent—a proportion exceeded by only eight towns in the sample. At the same date, 7·3 per cent of the population of Darlington in the 15-24 age group were in full-time education, which was below the national median, but still more than in other northern towns. The proportion for Gateshead, however, was only 5·4 per cent, which was well below even the northern median of 7·1 per cent. Now, it is of course true that the capacity of a local education authority to persuade parents to let their children stay on at school is limited. Nevertheless, one obvious course is to improve the quality of the secondary provision, as Gateshead did. But its resources for dealing with its problems were less than most towns, while the alternative claims on resources—for example, to raise housing standards—were greater. The number of council houses built per 1,000 population between 1945 and 1958 was 38—94 per cent of all houses erected in the town. This proportion was exceeded by only four of the 157 towns in the sample. Darlington, by contrast, built 32 council houses per 1,000 people—exactly the same as the national and northern median figures. They constituted 73·5 per cent of all houses built during that period—a proportion close to the national, but substantially below the northern, median.

	DARLINGTON		GATESHEAD		National
	Value	Rank	Value	Rank	Median
Economic character					
% in manufacture, etc.	47·8	62	56·5	39	41·6
% in service industries	32·9	104	27·9	127	37·4
Job ratio	105	58	88	102	99
Commuting ratio	24	141	69	58	51
Retail sales per head, 1950	159	40	88	134	125
Social Class					
% in social classes I+II	15·2	88	10·6	144	15·8
% in social classes IV+V	26·5	72	34·2	26	26·0
Voting					
General elections:					
1951 poll	87·1	13	84·7	56	83·7
1955 poll	82·3	17	75·7	112	78·0
1951 % voting left	49·2	84	60·7	19	49·6
1955 % voting left	47·4	89	60·6	16	48·8
Local elections, 1956-58					
% voting in contested elections	46	40	33	136	41
% uncontested seats	30	40	8	87	11
Health					
Infant mortality rate, 1950-2	29	67	44	3	28
Infant mortality rate, 1955-7	31	11	29	27	23
T.B. notification rate, 1957	95	67	171	3	88
Mortality rate, bronchitis 1957	106	78	163	23	106
Education, 1951					
% with terminal education age under 15	72·9	47	82·4	9	67·8
% aged 15-24 in full-time education	7·3	100	5·4	146	8·1

(*Source*: C. A. Moser & W. Scott, *British Towns*, 1961.)

The statistics suggest that a comparable drive to reduce infant mortality was going on in Gateshead. By the indicators for health, Darlington was a far better place to live than Gateshead in the 1950s. The tuberculosis notification rate for Gateshead was 171—the third worst for any town in the sample. The bronchitis mortality rate was 161 —the twenty-third in the table. Darlington, with 106, was equal to the national median, and well below the northern figure of 146. In 1950-2, the infant mortality figures reflected the general picture. The Gateshead figure was 44 —lower only than Rhondda and Rochdale in the entire sample—whereas that for Darlington—28—was close to the national, and well below the northern, medians. By 1955-7, however, against a national and regional downward trend, infant mortality actually rose in Darlington. Meanwhile, in Gateshead, there was a dramatic fall to 29 as compared with the northern median of 28 (Moser & Scott, 45).

The social structure of the towns was very much what might be guessed from the housing statistics. With 15·2 per cent in social classes I and II, Darlington was close to the national median and rather above the northern median. The corresponding figure for Gateshead was 10·6 per cent—well below the national, and even the northern, median. The proportions of the population in social classes IV and V were, not surprisingly, exactly opposite. With 26·5 per cent, Darlington was well below the northern median of 30·9 per cent (Moser & Scott, 44) and only fractionally higher than the national median. With 34·2 per cent, Gateshead was substantially higher than the northern, and well above the national, median. The distribution of the working population corresponded with the social structure. A much higher proportion of Gateshead's workers were in manufacturing etc., and fewer in the service industries. In both cases, there was a wide divergence from the medians in the case of Gateshead, a narrow one in that of Darlington. The job ratio—that

20

is to say, the population working in an area per 100 resident-occupied population—brings out a different kind of contrast between the towns. The figure for Darlington was 105 per cent, indicating a net influx of workers into the town each day. This is in line with its character as a relatively self-contained community, surrounded by residential villages. The job ratio for Gateshead was 88 per cent, showing a net outflow of workers, which is not surprising in an area bordering on the centre of one of the country's major industrial conurbations. The commuting ratio bears out this impression. Defined as the sum of the daily inflow and daily outflow, it tends to be low in the case of self-contained towns and high in parts of conurbations. It was 24 for Darlington, as against 69 for Gateshead.

Voting statistics for the two towns reflect their social and industrial structure. The proportion of the electorate in Darlington voting Left was close to 50 per cent in both 1951 and 1955, while in Gateshead it was fractionally over 60 per cent on both occasions. That is to say, politics in Darlington was highly competitive whereas Gateshead was safe for Labour. This was reflected at the local level, where the turn-out was above the national level in Darlington, but markedly below in Gateshead. In the former town, when there was a contest, voters had an incentive to go to the polls to put their own man in—or to keep the other side out. In the latter, on the other hand, the result in the great majority of cases, was a foregone conclusion; with the result that the individual's motive to record his vote was much reduced whatever his politics might be. One contrast appears puzzling at first sight: the turn-out at Darlington was higher, but so was the proportion of uncontested seats—the former seeming to indicate more interest, the latter more apathy, than at Gateshead. The explanation is that there was much more variety between one part of Darlington and another. Some wards were Labour strongholds, so that it seemed pointless to put up an opposition candidate, and vice versa. Gateshead was more uniform in character. Labour was so strong almost everywhere that its opponents had to put up candidates merely in order to keep their standard flying.

The character of the two boroughs can be summed up by saying that Gateshead is a town of extremes, whereas Darlington is moderate in almost all things. Moser & Scott's statistics cover 157 towns with populations over 50,000 as reflected in 60 variables, ranging from illegitimate births to the mortality rate for lung cancer. Darlington is among the nine towns closest to the median throughout all the variables. 'On average, one would expect each town to be outside the quartiles about ... thirty times' (Moser & Scott, 38-9). In fact, Darlington occupies such a position on only 12 occasions. It was a town which avoided the extremes of affluence and poverty, and where problems of health, housing and social provision were generally not acute. It was of balanced social and occupational character and fluctuated politically between the two main parties. Gateshead, on the other hand, was an extreme town, and several of the statistical eminences it occupied were bad ones. It fell outside the quartiles for 37 of the variables. It was a town of acute problems of many kinds, heavily dominated by one political party.

2
Darlington

The debate within the Labour Party

The first real move in the development of comprehensive secondary education in Darlington was made in January 1955. However, the issue was not finally resolved until more than twelve years later in October 1967. For some years before 1955 the local Labour Party had advocated the establishment of comprehensive education in municipal election manifestos but no attempt was ever made to realize the policy through the Labour Group on the Town Council. It was not only that Labour councillors were always in a minority before May 1956. An additional reason was that the Labour Council Group was unenthusiastic about the reorganization of secondary education. The older members particularly were content with the educational plan adopted in 1947, which provided for the development of bi-lateral schools—grammar technical and secondary modern technical. Each year the General Management Committee of the local Labour Party would insist on support for comprehensive education in the municipal election manifesto because it was national policy. But the members of the Labour Group could always stand on the Party rule that while the local Party laid down policy, timing and detailed implementation were matters solely for the Group to decide.

Discussion of the comprehensive education policy was eventually forced on Group members by the action of a former colleague. Even then, it was largely a discussion on tactics. The councillor, who had previously lost the Whip, put down a motion for discussion at the January 1955 meeting of the Town Council, which read simply: 'That this Council instructs the Education Committee to prepare plans for a comprehensive school in Darlington' (Council Min. LXIII, 6 January, 1955). The Labour Group determined that he should not be allowed to take the initiative and authorized the deputy leader to move an amendment:

> That this Council notes with satisfaction that the principle of the Comprehensive School is really being given effect to in the building of one school, as shown in the Educational Plan accepted by the Council, and further urges the Education Committee to give serious consideration to the extension of the principle by the provision of further facilities of this nature at the earliest appropriate date this can be made effective without damage or delay to the building programme to which we are now committed: also that copies of the Educational Plan be forwarded to all members of the Council who have been elected since the issue of such plan (*ibid.*).

The amendment was concerned not so much with educational policy as with taking the wind out of the dissident councillor's sails. It was designed to give the impression that the Labour Party had already done something about comprehensive schools: and that, in any case, the young councillor, who had only been a member of the authority for 18 months, did not really know what the educational plan of the Council was. In suggesting that the Council at the behest of the Labour minority was already building a comprehensive school, the amendment

24

was disingenuous. The school referred to was the Roman
Catholic Grammar School, then being enlarged to cater
for pupils from the Roman Catholic Secondary Modern
Boys' School, which was to be closed because of its
dilapidated condition. The combined school was to be
multi-lateral, not comprehensive, and had been decided
on by the Roman Catholic authorities through necessity
rather than principle. All the local authority did was to
approve the plan. The nature of the amendment was
recognized by the anti-Labour members of the Council,
who were totally against comprehensive schools. They
joined forces with the Labour Group to carry the amendment and defeat the original motion (*ibid.*). The Education Committee did not even bother to discuss the
amendment, and nothing was heard of comprehensive
schools for more than a year.

The opportunity for further discussion arose out of a
report on the 'Problems of Secondary Education in Darlington' submitted by the Chief Education Officer to the Education Committee in December 1955. The report dealt
mainly with the problems involved in the passing of the
post-war bulge in the school population from the primary
to secondary schools. It was also concerned, however,
with the development of technical courses in secondary
schools in accordance with the approved development
plan. After the report had been approved by the governing
bodies of the secondary schools concerned it was adopted
by the Education Committee. (Minute Qa 443, Education
Committee, 12 April, 1956.) But when the report came
before the full Council for approval, it was seen by certain Labour members to provide an opportunity of
re-opening the comprehensive school issue. The formerly
dissident councillor was back in the fold and was now
supported by a number of new additions to the Labour
Group, fresh and eager to carry out party policy. They
referred the report to the General Purposes Committee
(the whole council meeting in private) for consideration

(Council Min. LXXXII, 3 May, 1956), hoping that in the meanwhile a decision could be forced through the Labour Group. It proved even more beneficial than expected.

When next the Labour Group met, the municipal elections had intervened and the Labour Party was in control of the town for the first time ever. The militants took advantage of the new enthusiasm generated by electoral success and pressed their views on comprehensive schools. They succeeded in persuading a majority of the Group that the time had come to implement Labour policy. But, ominously, the minority included the two oldest and longest-serving members; the leader of the Group and the chairman of the Education Committee. (The Education Committee was one of several committees which had Labour chairmen even under an anti-Labour Council majority.) Both men were convinced that Darlington had the best possible system of education.

In spite of their opposition, the Group decided that when the report came before the General Purposes Committee it should be received with the reservation 'that the Education Committee be instructed to prepare a report on comprehensive schools ... with a view to the implementation of the Council's agreed policy at the earliest possible moment'. It had never been the Council's agreed policy, but the new Labour majority ensured the safe passage of the resolution (Min. P95, General Purposes Committee, 29 May, 1956). Four months later the Chief Education Officer produced a report for the Education Committee.

When the report first came before the Committee a decision was deferred for a month, ostensibly because members had received it only two days earlier. A more compelling reason may have been that there were a sufficient number of comprehensive school advocates present to carry their wishes, even allowing for three expected Labour abstentions. This was not the case at the next meeting of the Committee, and a decision was

26

taken to submit the report to the General Purposes Committee 'with a recommendation that the time is not appropriate to consider and develop comprehensive schools in Darlington' (Minute Qa 178, 15 November, 1956). But the reformers were not to be defeated so easily.

The peculiar organization of the Education Committee required that this recommendation had to be confirmed at a further meeting before it could be submitted to the General Purposes Committee. At this second meeting it was the practice to admit the Press. The chairman would read a statement of the decisions taken at the previous meeting and ask the members to confirm them. By convention, members did not move amendments, but on this occasion convention was broken. An amendment was moved and carried: 'That the report be submitted to the General Purposes Committee with a recommendation that the table showing how the existing and proposed schools could be organized as comprehensive schools be forwarded to the Minister of Education for his observations.' The amendment was deliberately moderate in tone so as to ensure maximum support and to prevent an adverse recommendation going from the Education Committee. It was successfully carried, in the face of opposition, through the General Purposes Committee and the Council (Council Min. LIX, 6 December, 1956). The report was sent to the Minister.

The Minister replied on 1 March, 1957, saying that, since reorganization would amount in law to the establishment of new schools, due notice would have to be given to the public, who would have the right to object. In view of this he did not want to say anything which might prejudice any future decision he might have to make. He advised the Authority that they would be wise to deal with current problems and wait until more experience was gained of other forms of secondary education. The Minister's letter was passed without comment from the Education Committee to the General Purposes

27

Committee. It was returned with a recommendation that 'this Authority seek the permission of the Minister of Education to vary the Education Development Plan to allow for the building of a Comprehensive School at Branksome' (Minute P104, G.P. Committee, 26 March, 1957). The intention behind this recommendation was to alter the plan for a bi-lateral school in a developing area of the town. It was thrown back by the Education Committee with a counter recommendation that 'the question be not considered at the present time' (Minute Qa 389, Ed. Committee, 11 April, 1957). Such a decision was again made possible by Labour abstentions.

This latest recommendation put the proponents of the new scheme in some difficulty, for in the public mind it would seem that the Education Committee should know more about education than the rest of the Council. Not to be defeated, they tried another approach. About this time the Leicestershire Council had decided on a new form of comprehensive secondary education and so the General Purposes Committee decided to defer a decision for one month while the Education Committee reconsidered the matter 'in the light of the recent decision of the Leicestershire Council' (Min. P120, G.P. Committee, 24 April, 1957). The matter was reconsidered on the basis of a report prepared by the Chief Education Officer on the Leicestershire scheme. It set out the pros and cons, but the general tenor suggested that the scheme was not suitable for Darlington. The Chief Education Officer had prepared a draft minute suggesting that the main thing was to push ahead with the existing development plan and that meanwhile other areas should be visited to gather information. It went on to say that the views of teachers' organizations and governing bodies should be sought. The comprehensive school enthusiasts saw this as a tactic to shelve the whole thing and refused to accept the draft resolution.

Instead they had carried: 'That without prejudice to

28

any future development of the educational system in the town on comprehensive lines the Education Committee advise the General Purposes Committee that in their opinion the Leicestershire scheme is not suitable for Darlington' (Min. Qa 57, 11 July, 1957). The purpose of this move was to keep the matter open and give time for further thought. Subsequently the Labour Group decided to switch the attack again. The idea this time was to reorganize two existing single-sex secondary modern schools as a co-educational comprehensive unit. The proposal was carried at the General Purposes Committee, where the comprehensive faction was stronger than on the Education Committee (G.P. Min. P23, 23 July, 1957).

After consultations with the head teachers of the two schools concerned and with the Schools Organizer, the Chief Education Officer submitted a report to the Education Committee. It was a factual report setting out how the schools could be adopted but leaving an overall impression that any such scheme would be very costly, difficult to achieve and in any case out of the question for at least five years because of the problems arising from the post-war bulge passing through the secondary schools. There was also the possibility of objections from parents to be considered and the effect of the proposal on the social balance of the grammar schools if one area of the town was excluded from the selection procedure. Not surprisingly, the Education Committee recommended:

(1) that no action be taken to convert the two Eastbourne Secondary Schools into a single comprehensive school; (2) that future action in this question be (a) that the views of local bodies, such as the Governors of maintained secondary schools and teachers' organizations ... be sought, (b) that a sub-committee be appointed to visit other areas where comprehensive schools have been established for a reasonable period ... [and] (c) that in the light of the information resulting ... a decision be taken as to whether the public notice of the

29

proposal to establish the Branksome Secondary School should be in respect of an instalment of a comprehensive school (Min. Qa 199, 14 November, 1957).

The Schools Organizer, in his recommendations to the Chief Education Officer, had strongly supported the idea of visiting other areas where comprehensive schools were established. He wanted a number of head teachers to accompany members of the Education Committee, or, alternatively, that the teachers' organizations should be urged to inform themselves at first hand of the problems involved. Unless something like this was done he doubted if the Darlington teachers could make an effective contribution to the issue, for too many teachers were victims of their own educational history and 'most teachers (and education officers) [were] too appreciative of the grammar school and too strongly affected by it to want to do anything against it'. The degree of consultation with the teachers, he thought, should depend upon the value of the advice they might offer (Memo. from Schools Organizer to C.E.O.).

These views of the Schools Organizer were not included in the report of the Chief Education Officer. In the event teachers went on expressing views against comprehensive schools without having first-hand knowledge and, at the same time, attacking councillors for knowing nothing about the matter. Much of this was done pseudonymously through letters to the local Press. Officially, the Chief Education Officer asked for the views of the National Union of Teachers (N.U.T.), the National Association of Schoolmasters (N.A.S.) and the Joint Four Secondary Association. The response of the latter organization was entirely predictable: they set out all the disadvantages of comprehensive schools and sang the praises of the grammar schools. The existing system of selection was considered 'sufficiently enlightened to serve the best interests of all the children of Darlington and ... the replacement of the successful and well established schools by an untried and educationally suspect system would have prejudicial effects upon the lives and careers of the children concerned'. These views were in line with an earlier unsolicited protest, signed by the deputy head and all members of the teaching staff of the Girls' High School. The N.U.T. took a similar line, with the substitution of the secondary modern for grammar schools. The N.A.S. was prepared to co-operate with a limited experiment. Its members preferred 'evolution to change' (Report by the C.E.O. on Secondary School Organization, August 1958).

During the time the views of the various organizations were being collated, seven members of the Education Committee, the Borough Architect, and the Chief Education Officer visited Walsall, West Bromwich and Coventry to gather information on secondary school reorganization. Six schools were visited but not one of them satisfied fully the definition of a comprehensive school; and none had been in existence long enough for a final assessment to be made. In the report that emerged from this inspection of other schools one head-master was quoted as saying: 'Come back in ten years' time and we will provide answers to all your questions.' He was also quoted as expressing the fear that comprehensive schools might never be as good as grammar schools and that under the then existing conditions they tended to have 'inferior staffs [and] inferior pupils' (Report to the Ed. Committee, 11 September, 1958). The greater part of the report was concerned with buildings and the areas served by the schools visited. It hardly dealt with the educational aspects of reorganization at all. Only one member of the delegation reported in favour of comprehensive schools, and he had been so inclined before the visit. Each member returned reinforced in his own prejudices.

In the light of the information collected, the Education Committee resolved:

That, without prejudice to any future review of the secondary school organization in Darlington, the public notice for the proposed Branksome Secondary School be in respect *initially* of a County Secondary Modern-Technical School ... and ... that ... the Borough Architect be requested to prepare plans which ... would enable the school to be the more readily adapted to any alternative organization which the Authority may decide upon in the future (Min. Qa 96, 11 September, 1958).

This was a skilfully worded minute, again drafted by the Chief Education Officer before the meeting. In spite of a Labour majority the only point gained by the comprehensive faction was the insertion of the word 'initially'.

They were far from satisfied and at the next meeting of the Labour Group, which was attended by less than half the members, more positive action was taken. Of 13 councillors present six were comprehensive school militants, five of the type to be swept along by a forceful discussion, and the Leader of the Group and the Chairman of the Education Committee both still opposed to comprehensive education. The views of the two 'elder statesmen' were disregarded and the Group decided to amend the Education Committee's recommendation when it came before the General Purposes Committee to read: 'That the public notice for the proposed Branksome Secondary School be in respect of a comprehensive school and that the Minister of Education be asked to vary the Development Plan accordingly.' This was to be a binding decision and all Group members were told by the Whips that they must support the amendment. The instruction was ignored by the Group Leader and the Education Committee Chairman but the amendment was carried through the General Purposes Committee and later confirmed by the Council. In the latter case the margin was only two votes; the leader of the Group abstained and the Education Committee Chairman voted against his Party.

32

Following the Council meeting attempts were made in the Labour Group to discipline the two elderly rebels. A majority of the Group refused to vote for the withdrawal of the Whip from them but it was agreed that they should be reprimanded. They refused to accept any such reprimand. Rather comically, motions were passed at subsequent meetings that the Leader be given a 'second reprimand' and that the Education Committee chairman be 'severely reprimanded' (Labour Group Minutes, 30 September, 1958 and 7 October, 1958). In an effort to gain support for his action, the Group Leader wrote to the General Secretary of the Labour Party, then Mr Morgan Phillips, but was told that members were expected to abide by Party policy. It was a matter for the Labour Group. On the basis of this advice the two men were asked if they were prepared to support Party policy. Neither would give an undertaking to do so. Because they were held in high esteem in the town their refusal put the Group in some difficulty. It was felt to be important to bring the two men into line because opponents were using the argument that not only was the Labour Group ignoring the advice of the Education Committee, but also that of its two most experienced members. They were asked to think over their attitude, but did not respond.

The public controversy

Meanwhile, opposition outside the Council was growing. The teachers' organizations were campaigning to have the Branksome decision reversed. Their attitude was reinforced rather than mollified by the public utterances of some Labour councillors, two of whom denied the teachers' right to consultation. One went so far as to accuse the grammar school masters of political prostitution! Even the N.A.S., which had originally declared itself willing to support a limited experiment, joined the campaign. It did so mainly because the Council had overruled the

Education Committee. A protest was sent to the Minister of Education and to the local Conservative Member of Parliament. The Member replied that he, too, had protested in their support and pointed out that the plan could not be effected without the Minister's approval. All objections would be carefully considered and he had no doubt that as soon as the 'notice is made by the Council you will be able to organize an effective objection from all your members'.

The notice was duly issued and pointed out that any ten or more local government electors for the area for which it was proposed to establish the school could object to the Ministry of Education within two months of its first publication. The teachers' and the old students' organizations of the two grammar schools went into action to organize the protest. The local Press was bombarded with letters and a petition was launched by the Old Girls' Association, rather tactlessly using the High School itself as a base. A Labour member seized on this to try and discredit the petition and asked the chairman of the Education Committee to 'enquire into the circumstances by which the premises at the Girls' High School are being used to further a campaign against the declared policy of the Authority'. Such an enquiry was made, and the Headmistress reflected that discretion would have been the better part of valour and was sorry that the Chairman had been additionally burdened. The Secretary of the Old Girls' Association objected 'most vehemently to the suggestion that their activities should be subject to censorship' when they were concerned in protecting the interests of the school to which they owed so much. In spite of these strong feelings the Labour member was assured by the Chief Education Officer that the situation would not recur. But the campaign went on and the petition was sent to the Minister of Education.

The Old Boys' Association took a half-page advertisement, headed 'Your Child's Future', in the local evening paper, to attack the Council's decision (*Northern Despatch*, 23 October, 1958). It outlined the benefits of a grammar school education, contained selective quotations against comprehensive schools and made great play with the opposition of the Labour Chairman of the Education Committee. The townspeople were urged to write to their M.P. and the Minister of Education. At the well-reported Old Boys' annual dinner, one member declared that:

> those who, with whatever good intent, would sweep away this heritage are still, however, subject to one all powerful deterrent. I do not mean the Minister, I do not even mean that much misunderstood power of the press or even the Party Whip. I refer to that much more potent force, the power which reposes in you and me, the ordinary people, the power of the ballot box.

He challenged one of the main Labour advocates of comprehensive education to fight him at the next municipal elections in the ward for which the new school was proposed.

Another speaker claimed that Darlington already had a system of education which was more comprehensive than any comparable or larger town in England. This was due mainly to the grammar school with its three-and-a-half centuries of tradition. He praised the Labour Chairman of the Education Committee, who was a man of 'knowledge and understanding—a man whom we can revere and respect in his attitude'. The real struggle was not over comprehensive schools but for power in the local Labour Party, and in which the children were merely pawns; they were cannon fodder. He asked: 'Have we been watching what is really a sham fight and is the real battle one for the control of the local Labour Party machine under which the younger elements wish to throw aside the older and wiser heads?' (*Northern Despatch*, 13 November, 1958). Such an assertion might have carried more weight had it come from someone other than this speaker who, in an

35

earlier local controversy, the fluoridation of water supplies, had discovered a 'Red plot'. A Labour member was quick to point this out in the letter columns of the local Press and suggested that this latest plot would be 'laughed out of court'.

The president of the Old Boys' Association said that, as he lived 150 miles away, he was unable to comment on the desirability of comprehensive schools in Darlington. However, if it meant the destruction of the grammar school he was opposed to the scheme, root and branch, and he would do anything he could to help! Members of the Association were urged to write to the Press, and this they did, disparaging the educational background of Labour members, attacking the Council for not heeding the Education Committee's advice, and the Labour Group for not respecting the views of its two most experienced members. Actually, their attack was a little inconsistent, for neither of the two men had had much formal education. The attacks worried the Labour Group, and at their next meeting it was decided 'that the Labour members of the Education Committee use the first available opportunity to re-affirm their belief in comprehensive schools' (Labour Group Minutes, 24 November, 1958). This was never done.

Even the Prime Minister was dragged into the controversy. Mr Macmillan was visiting Darlington on 13 January, 1959, and was supposed to have expressed a wish to pay an informal visit to the grammar school. The Education Committee agreed to make the necessary arrangements, and this raised a storm of protest from certain members of the Labour Group. While it was realized that the Prime Minister was not making a special visit to the town to put his weight behind the opposition to comprehensive schools, it was thought that the local Conservative Association was using the occasion for this purpose. Publicly the Association had hardly been involved in the controversy so far, because their supporters in the

Council sat as Independents. It had only recently begun to put forward official Conservative candidates. In any case, the Labour attack misfired and resolved itself into a squabble between the Labour mayor, who had to receive the Prime Minister, and a section of the Labour Group. The visit took place as planned but made little impact either way. A few weeks later, Mr Gaitskell visited the town. He did not visit the grammar school, but went instead to a secondary modern school!

The Ministry's attitude

On 5 February, 1959 the Ministry wrote asking a number of questions. The most important one was: 'would children living in the districts of Cockerton and Pierremont be excluded from the Authority's normal secondary selection arrangements?' In suggesting that the reply should be: 'if the Branksome Secondary School is organized on comprehensive lines then the pupils from county primary schools who live in the "catchment area" will not be considered in the authority's normal secondary school procedure,' the Chief Education Officer provoked a strong reaction from the anti-comprehensive school members of his Committee and the Council. It meant that children living in the area would not have the right to attend the grammar schools even if they reached the required standard. Feeling was strong that parents should have the unequivocal right to opt out for their children.

After the intervention of the Labour Group, the reply that went to the Minister stated that the authority would accept interim opting-out arrangements, but that ultimately there would be no choice. It was felt that to allow opting-out arrangements when the school was fully established would show little faith in the comprehensive principle. The Minister replied on 10 April, 1959 saying that he could not allow the proposed school to be organized as suggested. He referred to the heavy volume of objections and the ultimate disappearance of any right to opt out. Such restrictions could not be countenanced 'simply in order that a new comprehensive school may enjoy a monopoly of the abler children within its area'. The pro-comprehensive school faction failed to persuade a majority of the Education Committee to respond to this rebuff with a deputation to the Ministry, and the letter was simply received (Minutes Qa 344, 16 April, 1959 and Q 24, 27 April, 1959). Labour members were again divided.

Before these minutes came to the full Council for confirmation, the municipal elections intervened and Labour lost two seats. Both defeated councillors were ardent supporters of the comprehensive principle, one being the man who made the original move in 1955. However, in law, they remained councillors for four days after the elections and so were eligible to speak in the debate at the Council meeting held the day after their defeat at the polls. They still spoke strongly in favour of the proposed comprehensive school and called for a deputation to be sent to the Ministry. Anti-Labour councillors taunted the Labour Group with arguments that their answer was in the ballot box. As Labour members had claimed in the past that they had been elected into a majority position because of their comprehensive school policy, they could hardly complain.

Actually, the two Labour defeats could be explained partly by the national political position, for in May 1959 there was a national swing against the Labour Party. One of the seats lost was normally anti-Labour, but had been won in 1956 by the Labour Party against a weak candidate and when public opinion was more favourable to it. In the other case, the ward was marginal and tended to swing back and forth. The defeated councillor was a leading supporter, and he had been the subject of a virulent personal campaign. Further evidence that the Labour Party was not defeated on its school policy is seen in the fact that the very marginal ward in which

38

the school was to be situated was held, albeit with a
majority of only 93. In spite of all the arguments about
the ballot box, the Labour Party still had an overall
majority on the Council and the matter was referred
back to the General Purposes Committee.

Between these meetings the Labour Group decided that
a deputation should be sent to the Ministry (Labour Group
Minutes, 2 June, 1959). This decision was carried in the
General Purposes Committee, and subsequently the Education Committee appointed the Chairman, Vice-Chairman
and three pro-comprehensive members as their representatives. As it turned out, the Chairman and Vice-Chairman
were unable to attend and the deputation became one of
people who were all in favour of comprehensive schools.
The deputation was accompanied by the Chief Education
Officer, who was not in favour. Ministry officials were
pressed for information on the number of objections to
the scheme, and the deputation was told these numbered
2,500. Apart from the question of opting out there was
little difference between the Ministry and the authority.
The officials took the view that, provided parents were
allowed freedom of choice, secondary education could be
organized in any way the authority pleased. The deputation reported back accordingly, and the Education Committee went on to consider two schemes. One, proposed
by the three members of the deputation, maintained the
comprehensive principle, balancing a right to opt out with
a right extended to parents of children outside the catchment area to opt in. The other, skilfully put forward
by the Chief Education Officer as a compromise, suggested up-grading all secondary moderns to include G.C.E.
streams, a proposition he had argued against four years
earlier. He again suggested that before a decision was
taken there should be consultations with the Teachers'
Advisory Committee, teachers' organizations and school
governing bodies. All these endorsed the scheme, as did
the Council. The Labour Group seemed glad to put an

39

end to the controversy and supported the new scheme as a victory for common-sense. Only one Labour member opposed the scheme, and he was the man who won the marginal ward in which the comprehensive school was to have been built. Ironically, he was 'put on the carpet' by the Labour Group. In May 1960 Labour lost control to an Independent-Conservative alliance and nothing further was done until it was regained three years later.

The Peter Plan

Perhaps the most important development during the three years was the apparent conversion of the Chief Education Officer to the comprehensive principle. He was aware that, in the changing climate of opinion, and given the likelihood of Labour returning to power both locally and nationally, comprehensive education would come, and that it was his duty as a good administrator to be prepared. In any case it was becoming necessary to re-examine the development of secondary education in the town for practical reasons. For example, it was increasingly difficult for the Boys' Grammar School to contain the phenomenal growth in its sixth-form numbers without building a completely new school. When the comprehensive ball started rolling again shortly after Labour regained control of the Council in May 1963 he was ready. At a meeting of the Education Committee on 22 July he was asked 'to prepare a report ... on the selection for, and the organization of secondary education' (Minute Q117, 22 July, 1965). Within two months, including the holiday period, such a report was presented to the Committee.

The Labour councillor credited with this new initiative had not previously consulted his colleagues, and there had been no discussion in the Labour Group. For some reason, the new Labour Chairman of the Committee, a long-standing advocate of comprehensive education, had decided to make no move until the September meeting. Perhaps he was playing himself in first. There is a hint of rivalry as to who should be the first on the ball. The move may have been sparked off by earlier discussions on the feasibility of introducing modern language courses into secondary modern schools and the news of Ministry approval for the building of a secondary school in the 1964-5 programme. Whatever the background, the occasion of the decision seems to have been a confused one. Conservative members complained afterwards that they could not remember any such decision being taken. At least one Labour member shared their doubts, but as he favoured the move, he did not mind. What may have happened is that the Chief Education Officer put a rather garbled proposition into coherent form, a not unusual occurrence in committee work.

That the situation was confused is apparent from the motion, discussed at the Council meeting on 5 September, 1963: 'That this Council as education authority for Darlington, believing that the eleven-plus selection test discriminates against all but the most fortunate child, abolish the eleven-plus selection test and instruct the Chief Education Officer to prepare a scheme to this effect.' The motion was lost. It was moved by an erstwhile Labour councillor, who had had the Whip withdrawn, a situation reminiscent of the very first move in 1955. But the most interesting aspect is that the motion was seconded by the Councillor who had re-opened the issue at the July meeting of the Education Committee. If he realized that he was already on the way to getting what he wanted, why second this new move?

Seven days after this motion was defeated in Council the Chief Education Officer produced his report. It proposed to abolish the eleven-plus, to set up seven neighbourhood, co-educational comprehensive schools, catering for children between the ages 11-16, and one sixth-form college. Such a scheme aimed to ensure that all secondary schools would have a full cross-section of the ability range, be able to develop courses up to G.C.E. 'O' level standard, and also to organize courses suited to their special interest.

While the proposals necessitated the physical and academic equalization of all secondary schools, they allowed the continued use of existing facilities, and so minimized the expense involved in the changeover. The report recognized that some people might argue that the grammar schools would be destroyed. It suggested, however, that their best traditions would be preserved in the sixth-form college, which would occupy the buildings of the existing Boys' Grammar School and be 'equipped to meet in full measure the needs of the more able pupils'. This arrangement would also facilitate the retention, concentration and more effective use of highly qualified staff. A further advantage of the scheme was the possibility of developing a higher education campus based on the sixth form college, the teacher training college, and the college of further education, all in close proximity to one another. The Chief Education Officer recommended that there should be 'full and detailed consultation with all the interests affected', and that the scheme should be introduced gradually over a five-year period. He emphasized that he was merely explaining the problems and making 'tentative suggestions for dealing with them' and wanted as much publicity as possible so that there would be a better chance of 'producing a worthwhile revision' of the authority's Development Plan (Report of C.E.O., September 1963).

On receipt of the report the Education Committee resolved : 'That the report ... be forwarded to all members of the Council ... [and] that the views of all interested bodies such as School Governors and Teachers' Organizations on the proposals be sought' (Min. Q144, 12 September, 1963). The report was issued to the local Press, and both morning and evening papers ran full-scale articles on its contents. It was dubbed the Peter Plan after its author, a title that stuck.

Consultation with interested bodies

By early January 1964, governing bodies, the N.U.T., the N.A.S., the Head Teachers' Association, the Joint Four Secondary Association (a federation of the four predominantly grammar-school teachers' associations), and the co-opted member of the Education Committee, who was Principal of Darlington Training College, had all submitted views on the scheme to the Chief Education Officer. They were considered by the Education Committee at a special meeting on 27 January, together with comments on them by the Chief Education Officer. Only one elected member seems to have troubled to prepare a written critique of the Plan, but it was never considered by the Committee. Nor was it considered by the Labour Group, of which he was a member. It was, however, read by his colleague, the Chairman of the Education Committee; no doubt, too, the author had something to say on it in committee. Memoranda were also submitted by the old pupils' associations of the two grammar schools and the Grammar School Association, a body mainly composed of parents of grammar school boys.

The Chief Education Officer reported that his Plan had received strong support from the three governing bodies covering the town's secondary modern schools. It found less favour with the fourth, which was responsible for the grammar schools. Similarly, the Joint Four Secondary Association, with membership mainly drawn from the grammar schools, objected to the proposals. Its objections were echoed by the associations connected with these schools. The other three teachers' organizations and the Teachers' Advisory Committee were less critical, and all favoured at least some aspects of the Plan. None of these bodies put forward a complete alternative scheme,

43

although the co-opted member of the Education Committee made a bold attempt to do so. She suggested six comprehensive schools, catering for children between 12 or 13 to 16+, each developing particular specialisms, and arranged to give a choice between single-sex and mixed schools.

The majority of the N.U.T. would have preferred 11-18 comprehensives, though there was some support for a continuation of the existing pattern, retaining the eleven-plus but with the grammar school intake reduced from $22\frac{1}{2}$-25 per cent to 10-$12\frac{1}{2}$ per cent. The grammar school governors and the Joint Four suggested that alternative schemes should be considered, including the Leicestershire Plan, which they had rejected in the earlier controversy. The Joint Four also thought 'the answer may be in dealing more successfully with the problems left after the obvious selection has been made'. This might be done 'by fuller implementation of the 1958 scheme for transfers between schools'; this was another scheme which had not been too appealing to some of them when first mooted. It was suggested that there might be difficulty in staffing the new schools with graduates when there was no sixth form to attract them. In a sudden surge of social conscience, attention was also drawn to the 'wide cross-section' of pupils attending the grammar schools, which it was thought would be broken down by the institution of neighbourhood comprehensives. All in all, the Joint Four remained 'convinced that there already exists in Darlington the framework of a system of education far more "comprehensive" than anything the new scheme could produce' (Report to the Education Committee, January 1964). This was a view which had not changed since the 1950s.

The possible difficulties of staffing and the claimed social breadth of the grammar schools intake were arguments the Chief Education Officer had previously used to ward off comprehensive schools. But he now argued that

44

the situation had changed. If graduates were not prepared to teach in the schools, and he thought they
would be, there were plenty of three-year-trained teachers
leaving the training colleges to fill the gap. So far as the
social balance of the schools was concerned, the catchment area could be so drawn as to ensure there was no
problem. In any case, he argued, the problem would not
arise because of the way in which new housing was being
developed in various parts of the town. Eventually it
was agreed that parents could opt for which-ever school
they preferred for their children. The vast majority opted
for their neighbourhood school.

Many of the doubts expressed by those who accepted
the principles of the Plan related to the size of the proposed schools. As originally conceived there were to be
seven schools each with less than 800 pupils. It was
objected that these would not be viable comprehensive
units able to offer a sufficiently wide range of subjects.
The Chief Education Officer conceded that some revision might be necessary, and in the scheme finally approved
by the Education Committee the seven five-form entry
schools gave way to six eight-form entry schools with
rolls, ultimately, of 1170. The main factor in this decision was the proposal in the Hailsham Report on the
North-East (Cmd. 2206, November 1963) that Darlington
should be regarded as a 'growth point' within a development area and so could look forward to having an expand-
ing economy and increasing population. On this basis
the Borough Surveyor projected a growth in population
of one-third, giving a total of 112-115,000 by 1981.

The inability of the officials to give any precise details
of the stages by which this population increase would be
achieved led one Labour councillor to remark that 'Hailsham is speculative. The Borough Surveyor presents us
with speculation at one remove. The Chief Education
Officer's estimates are conjecture upon speculation at
one remove!' Nevertheless the figures were accepted as

45

the basis for the future pattern of secondary school organization. The Education Committee also decided to set up a Joint Committee with representatives of the teachers' organizations 'for the purpose of considering the scheme in detail and submitting proposals for its implementation'. Since at the same time the scheme was 'approved in principle' and it was to be submitted at once to the Minister, it seems clear that only a very restricted role was envisaged for the Committee (Minute Q378, 27 January, 1964).

Such a view is confirmed in the defeat of a move by a Conservative councillor to postpone a vote in the Committee until the teachers had made a 'decision' on the Plan. The chairman stated that:

> Policy is made by lay members, the professionals advise. This is democracy as we know it; this is government both locally and nationally. We are the only people who can take a decision on this ... We have consulted them, and we asked them to give us the minority views as well as the majority ... We decide the policy, the administrators have to put it into practice and find answers to problems ...

Of the opposition, a sole Conservative councillor agreed with the chairman and his Labour colleagues. He failed to persuade the remaining members of the Independent and Conservative Group to his view that they should 'disregard sectional interest' and voted alone with the Labour members (*Northern Despatch*, 28 January, 1964). Unlike 1958, when the previous scheme was submitted, Labour was now not only in control but virtually united. The former leader still served on the Committee, and still had his doubts, but he was now too old to contend against the majority.

In the days leading up to the next full Council meeting when the Committee's decisions had to be confirmed, the local Press again provided a forum for debate. It was a much more balanced debate than that which took place in the 1950s. The newspapers themselves published

46

a wealth of factual information and it seemed that there were now a greater number of interested and articulate people in favour of comprehensive education, especially the Peter Plan version, than had previously been the case. On the night of the Council debate the local evening paper published an editorial urging councillors to 'probe deep' before taking an 'irrevocable step' and asserting the right of parents to be considered (*Northern Despatch*, 6 February, 1964). But as the Labour Group had already agreed to support the Education Committee's decisions and that only the Committee chairman should speak (Labour Group Minutes, 4 February, 1964), the debate was probably something of an anti-climax.

Conservative councillors attacked the scheme as 'the view of one man and one man alone' and 'a brilliant intellectual exercise, but not a practical proposition', as well as voicing all the predictable arguments about the destruction of the grammar schools. They echoed many of the sentiments of those interest groups in favour of the *status quo*, although there is no evidence of formal contacts between them. It was to no avail, for after a 'massive documentary' exposition of the Plan by its Chairman, the Education Committee's decisions were endorsed by 23 votes to 15 (Council Minute LVII, 6 February, 1964). One Labour member, the former leader, abstained and the Conservative member who had voted with the Labour Group in committee did so again in council. In doing so, the latter had withstood considerable pressure from Party colleagues and from individuals connected with the grammar schools.

During the following months, the controversy flared intermittently, in the main going over old ground and coming from the same sources. One interesting new development was the raising of a petition in support of the scheme by the Education Committee Chairman. It upset the staffs of the grammar schools, who questioned the ethics of such procedure. The purpose of the petition

47

was to act as a countervailing force to any repeat of the 1959 petition against comprehensive education, which had been a factor in the Minister's rejection of the authority's proposals. In the event, the Chairman's petition was never used. Presumably it was not thought necessary.

On 12 March, 1964 the Education Committee considered an invitation from the Ministry to discuss the Peter Plan. It was decided to send the Committee's Chairman and Vice-Chairman, both Labour and in favour of the proposals, the Conservative who had supported them, one Conservative who was very much against, and the co-opted member, who was in favour but with certain reservations (Minute Q459, 12 March, 1964). Before the visit, which took place on 5 June, 1964, they were supplied with a comprehensive brief by the Chief Education Officer, something he had not done for the 1959 deputation. He also armed himself with information from two authorities developing similar schemes who had already been to the Ministry. As with these two authorities no definite pronouncement was made by the Ministry on the Darlington Plan. The deputation left with the feeling that the Ministry was not anxious to give an early decision with a General Election in the offing. In closing the meeting one official commented, 'I was merely bowling to see how you batted'. The authority was asked to keep the Ministry informed of the Joint Committee discussions (Report to Ed. Committee June 1964).

At the time of the Ministry meeting the Joint Committee had not met because of delay in reaching agreement with some of the teachers' organizations on its constitution. It was eventually agreed that it should comprise:

5 representatives of the Education Committee;
9 secondary heads (i.e. all those involved, but excluding the heads of Roman Catholic schools);
3 primary heads;

9 secondary assistant teachers.

Teachers' organizations were invited to submit nominations as follows:

	N.U.T.	Joint Four	N.A.H.T.	N.A.S.
Secondary Heads	5	2	1	1
Primary Heads	2	—	1	—
Secondary Assistants	5	2	—	2

The Education Committee accepted these recommendations and also decided that the Joint Committee should have power to co-opt, a provision which was later used to bring in three assistant teachers from primary schools.

The *Ad Hoc* Committee, as it became known, met for the first time on 20 July, 1964 and elected the Chairman of the Education Committee to preside over it. Arising from a report of the visit to the Ministry of Education the Committee decided that its first discussions should be on the following matters (Minutes of *Ad Hoc* Committee, 20 July, 1964):

1. Losses and gains to the present secondary schools likely to result from the proposed changes.
2. Maintenance of comparable standards, including staffing, in the proposed schools.
3. Opportunities for (a) late developers to take G.C.E. at O level and (b) pupils to stay on at school beyond the age of 16 without necessarily taking A level.
4. Standards required for admission to the sixth-form college.
5. Zoning of the proposed schools and possibility of social segregation.
6. Whether all schools should be co-educational.
7. Timing of the implementation of the scheme.

The first of these topics was discussed at the Committee's next meeting on 26 September, 1964. Six members had responded to an invitation from the Chief Education

Officer to submit their views in writing in advance of the meeting. These had been drawn together in a kind of balance sheet as a basis for discussion, though no attempt had been made to evaluate the pros and cons. Of course, the written submissions would have allowed the Chief Education Officer to marshal his arguments in advance. Discussion at this meeting was prolonged, and it was eventually resolved to resume the topic at the next meeting. Before it took place, however, the Committee visited schools in four other areas. At the second meeting the Committee still failed to reach the end of the first of the seven points.

The Chief Education Officer submitted a memorandum which indicates some exasperation with the slow rate of progress. He reminded the Committee that: 'The Authority has accepted the Plan in principle' and suggested that there was no point 'in merely going over old ground'. The real function of the Committee was 'to consider the proposals in detail and to advise the Authority on their implementation. If the committee felt that the comprehensive principle was not sound, it should say so.... In that event there would be little point in this committee continuing to meet.' If, on the other hand, the Committee accepted the comprehensive principle, they should get down to the consideration of detail, reporting to the Education Committee any points they considered had been overlooked (Memo to *Ad Hoc* Committee from C.E.O., 19 October, 1964).

Whether or not this memorandum was directed at their representatives, the Joint Four Secondary Association submitted a reply to the next meeting of the Committee. The Association felt able to 'distinguish very clearly between the comprehensive principle and particular types of school organization', and so the Chief Education Officer's suggested 'affirmation' was 'quite unnecessary'. Agreement or disagreement with the authority's decision in no way affected the Association's duty or willingness to

50

advise the Committee. It was a 'professional obligation' to see that whatever system was adopted should be made to work as successfully as possible. The absence of any previous experience made a critical approach essential (Memo to C.E.O., 6 November, 1964). This exchange, though sharp, served a useful purpose and the Committee thereafter split into three sub-committees, each taking two of the outstanding points on the agenda. From then on, business moved much faster; sub-committees prepared reports which were discussed in plenary sessions and then, in each case, accepted as 'representing accurately the views of the Committee'. The Committee completed its deliberations on 12 April, 1965 (Minutes of 8th Meeting of *Ad Hoc* Committee, 12 April, 1965). While it had never been the intention that the Committee should alter the Plan, it had been able to point out many of the problems which would be involved in its implementation. In a covering note with their report, Committee members told the Education Committee that they were 'appreciative of the opportunity they have been given to examine and comment on the authority's proposals', and thanked the Chairman for the 'very pleasant and efficient manner in which the meetings had been conducted'. The Education Committee reciprocated by sending a letter of thanks to each member of the Committee.

Approval of the Peter Plan by the Secretary of State

After approval by the Education Committee, the report prepared by the *Ad Hoc* Committee was passed on to the Department of Education and Science for the views of the Secretary of State. There was no immediate reply, and so the Chief Education Officer wrote again on 9 August, 1965, reminding the Department that the proposals had first been submitted eighteen months earlier and that all the additional information asked for had been supplied. As the Plan was in line with one of the methods of secondary reorganization described in Circular 10/65, the authority hoped that early acceptance of the scheme might be forthcoming. The plea was successful, and approval came on 16 August, 1965. The Secretary of State welcomed the authority's proposals and said he was impressed by the careful consideration which had clearly been given to the various aspects of the scheme. He did not wish to raise any questions of principle, although he did ask that particular attention be given to staffing arrangements (letter from D.E.S. to L.E.A., 16 August, 1965). The Education Committee welcomed the decision and resolved to begin implementing the plan from September 1967; this was confirmed in full Council by 20 votes to 8 after a half-hearted attempt by the Conservatives to prevent the scheme going through. In the Council discussion the Conservative Leader said: 'I realize I am bashing my head against a brick wall' (*Northern Despatch*, 8 October, 1965).

Roman Catholic secondary schools

There still remained the problem of fitting the Roman Catholic secondary schools into the proposed comprehensive pattern. A number of meetings took place between the Chief Education Officer and R.C. authorities at which five possible schemes were considered. Only three of these were regarded as viable propositions, and it was left to the church authorities to determine which they preferred. Eventually it was decided to convert the R.C. Secondary School for Boys, the multi-lateral school referred to earlier, into a seven-form entry co-educational school catering for pupils from 11-18. It contrasted with the proposals for the majority of the town's children in that sixth-form work would be an integral part of the school. On 13 April, 1966 the Bishop of Hexham and Newcastle confirmed this plan, and the Chief Education Officer passed the news on to the Department of Education and Science. The secretary of State endorsed the R.C. plan in May 1967, and with this the main outline of Darlington's comprehensive policy was complete.

Postscript

In May 1967 the Conservatives regained control of the Town Council. As they had promised in statements and election addresses since 1964 to re-examine the secondary reorganization proposals 'with a view to retaining' the grammar schools, a shadow was cast over the whole Peter Plan conception. The outlook brightened, however, when, at the first meeting of the Education Committee after the municipal elections, Conservative members unanimously supported a decision to proceed with £300,000 worth of alterations at the Girls' High School as part of the initial phase of implementing the Plan (Min. Q18, 8 June, 1967). Labour members, who had come to the meeting prepared for a 'bitter fight', were surprised and delighted with the outcome; one being moved to declare 'the fight is over' (*Northern Echo*, 10 June, 1967). But it was not; it was only postponed.

Shortly after this meeting, in a municipal by-election, the Conservatives renewed their pledge to preserve the grammar schools. They informed the electorate, in what was a safe Conservative ward, that 'having only taken marginal control of the Council ... it would be wrong to impose immediate new plans'. Nevertheless, it was intended to replace the previous plan, which had been 'adopted and discussed for a very long time ... with a better, modern and well considered scheme'. Under consideration was a plan to develop 'two comprehensive type units teaching to O level [and] two comprehensive schools teaching to A level/University entrance'. The grammar schools would be kept but the intake reduced (by-election address, 22 June, 1967).

Labour members reacted strongly and promised to fight the proposals all along the line. Strong criticism also came from the local evening paper, which described them in an editorial as a 'contradiction in terms'. It was not possible to cream off some pupils for the grammar schools and still call the remaining schools comprehensive. The editorial suggested that the 'Tories seem to be getting into a mess on education, largely because they don't seem to have done their homework' (*Northern Despatch*, 20 June, 1967). True or not, the local Conservatives were determined to block further progress of the Peter Plan. At the next full Council meeting the Chairman of the Education Committee withdrew the minute sanctioning the alterations to the Girls' High School.

This move was described by his Vice-Chairman as a 'planned withdrawal', the purpose of which was to give time for further consideration. It was felt that many objections and criticisms of the Peter Plan had been too hastily overridden and 'that the composition of the various bodies which discussed the Plan was heavily loaded in favour of the Labour members' (*Northern Despatch*, 7 July 1967). There is no evidence at all to substantiate this charge, but what the Vice-Chairman probably had in mind became clearer later when his Chairman stated that 'it was well known that 80 per cent of all teachers are socialists' (interview with writer, 1 August, 1967) and that the N.U.T. has a 'permanent socialist majority' (*Northern Despatch*, 22 September, 1967). Yet it was their intention to submit the new proposals, when they had been fully worked out, to the teachers for consideration. It did not seem to occur to the Chairman that if his assertions were true, any committee of teachers would probably be hostile to his plans. Both Chairman and Vice-Chairman were inexperienced newcomers to local government, and the former Labour Chairman expressed the views of many people when he said 'it appears that the Conservatives had no idea of what they were passing' in the Education

Committee. He promised to 'lead a campaign in the town' (*Northern Despatch*, 7 July, 1967).

Together with two of his colleagues he used the standing orders to call a special meeting of the Education Committee. But to no avail; the action of the Conservative Chairman was endorsed. At a further meeting the Education Committee explicitly reversed its previous decision to alter the Girls' High School and decided to reconvene the *Ad Hoc* Committee to 'review the plan for secondary education in an effort to improve the plan in the light of present-day knowledge and experience, it being clearly understood that any improvement must conform to the principles of comprehensive education' (Min. Q76, 13 July, 1967). The reference to comprehensive education was included at the insistence of Labour members, but, as they were outnumbered at the meeting, they could do nothing about the overall decision. In any case, it was not regarded as a concession by the Conservative chairman, who claimed that he was 'as much in favour of comprehensive education as anyone' and could see 'nothing anomalous in maintaining the grammar schools alongside comprehensive schools' (interview with writer, 1 August, 1967). At the next full Council meeting, the Labour Group attempted to revert to the original Plan but were defeated by two votes. The lone Conservative councillor who supported Labour members on an earlier occasion did so again (Council Min. XX14, 24 August, 1967).

By now the controversy was again raging. The local papers were taking an openly hostile line and constantly nagging at the Conservatives for their inept attempts to go back on the Peter Plan. Editorials suggested that the educational argument had been won and that the question was now getting 'bogged down in a party political slanging match'. There was praise for the Conservative councillor who had voted against his colleagues and quotations from a speech by Mr Heath, which welcomed the movement away from selection at eleven-plus (*Northern*

Despatch, 22 August, 1967). The Conservatives were said to 'have their backs to the wall' and 'did not appear to understand what they were saying' (*Northern Despatch*, 25 August, 1967). A Labour councillor asked the Leader of the Opposition to use his influence with local Conservatives, and also wrote to the Secretary of State for Education. Mr Heath refused to intervene and Mr Gordon Walker promised to watch the situation carefully. The constituency's Labour M.P. promised the Conservatives a relentless fight, and in return was attacked for interfering in local affairs. It was conveniently forgotten that the boot was on the other foot in the 1950s. In any case, the prospective Conservative candidate was currently engaged in attacking the Peter Plan. As the argument developed, even pro-Peter Plan grammar school teachers showed their support for the first time by writing to the local papers. Their aim was to dispel the idea that the whole of the grammar schools' staffs were opposed to the Plan.

Perhaps the most interesting development was the emergence of a Parents' Action Committee to fight for the Peter Plan. It started from a move in the local Labour Party initiated by a member who was a grammar school teacher. As the teacher did not want to play an open part in the Committee, the former Labour chairman of the Education Committee offered to undertake the organizing work. He asked Labour members 'not to tie his hands by making the Committee too political' (Labour Party G.M.C. Minute, 19 July, 1967). Always a man of his word, he immediately set about recruiting people, sometimes adopting quite bold methods, at least for a normally reserved man. For example, whenever a letter appeared in the local Press attacking the Conservatives' attitude he would call on the writer, explain the aims of the Committee and ask for his support. Soon, by this method and by direct invitation to individuals and organizations, a widely based Committee, both socially and politically, was built up.

Politically, the bulk of members were probably Labour Party sympathizers, but there was at least one possible Communist and several Conservatives. Socially, it included labourers, craftsmen, trade union organizers, teachers, an insurance executive, a training officer, a doctor, a managing director and a master builder. The master builder is interesting in that he had twice opposed Labour candidates in local elections. He joined the Committee after attending an Education Committee meeting and being 'disgusted at the shambles the Conservatives were producing in their search for a policy'. The Conservative councillor who had opposed his colleagues was approached to join but refused because he thought the Committee was too closely identified with the Labour Party. This did not protect him from the wrath of his fellow Conservative councillors, who attempted to expel him from their Group. He saved them the trouble by resigning from the Council.

The Committee provoked the formation of another committee dedicated to the retention of the grammar schools. It was organized from among 'people who were known to have children at the Grammar School and High School' (*Northern Despatch*, 22 September, 1967). The Parents' Action Committee appears to have been the more active in holding meetings and propagating its views, although it did have the advantage of a sympathetic local Press. So much so that a member of the Committee was given considerable space to write an article in support of the Peter Plan. As a family man with a son at grammar school, twins at secondary modern school, and a daughter in the transitional stage, he was regarded as ideal for such an assignment. In a telling piece he wrote of his conversion to the Peter Plan from a strongly antagonistic position (*Northern Despatch*, 1 October, 1967).

Meanwhile the Conservatives' alternative was under consideration. It was being prepared by three 'key members' : the Chairman and Vice-Chairman of the Education

Committee and the Chairman of the local Association, a former councillor. There does not seem to have been any formal consultation with interested outside bodies, but the Committee Chairman has said that he 'took all the advice he could get hold of' and that casual contacts with individual teachers and the like were 'turned to good advantage' (interview with writer, 1 August, 1967). When the proposals did appear, they got virtually no support from any of the teachers' organizations, not even the Joint Four. Nor did the governing bodies support them, except, of course, for the one covering the grammar schools. The Conservatives proposed:

1. Retention of the town's two grammar schools but with substantially reduced numbers.
2. One comprehensive school catering for children between the ages of 12-18.
3. Three comprehensive 'type' schools catering for children between the ages of 12-16.
4. Entry to all secondary schools at 12.
5. Selection to be based on 'a profile attainment estimation system at primary schools governed by parental choice'.

(*Amendments—Secondary Education Re-organization*, September 1967.)

There had been a good deal of confusion in education circles and among many parents during the period of waiting for the Conservative proposals. Publication made the situation worse; especially as the teachers' organizations and the Chief Education Officer advised that they were impracticable. Even if they could be implemented it would take time, and meanwhile there would be the problem of allocating pupils to secondary schools. The proposals suggested that allocation should be based on school records, teachers' recommendations and parental choice. This method was rejected by the majority of

teachers either because it was thought that parental choice
was incompatible with selection or because they preferred
not to be responsible for making the necessary recommendations. Conservative members were reluctant to
accept the teachers' views, but were warned by the Chief
Education Officer that not to do so would involve a very
serious decision. Even a Labour member who, in the
1950s, had scorned the teachers' views now thought that
professional advice should be considered and that the
teachers should not be forced to act against their will.
After two bitter and stormy meetings the Education Committee decided by one vote to retain the eleven-plus as an
interim measure for one year. It was a decision which
brought even greater protests. But it was also the beginning of the end. For at the next full Council meeting,
after an abortive attempt by Labour members to revert
to the Peter Plan, the Conservatives surprisingly offered
to discuss the matter. After some initial uncertainty among
Labour members about what such a meeting would discuss, the Tory Plan or the Peter Plan, the offer was
accepted.

The climb-down really started two nights earlier when
the Conservative Group had decided that their proposals
were unlikely to be accepted and that they would probably have to accept the Peter Plan. But between this
meeting and the Council meeting the Education Committee Chairman called on the former Labour Chairman,
apparently to try and reach some accommodation. He
was rebuffed. It was the intention of Labour members to
force the issue and to keep the Conservatives at the
Council meeting all night if necessary. It was not necessary. Following the Council meeting, in a midnight statement to the Press, the Conservative Chairman made it
clear that his Party's capitulation was complete. He
said it would have been possible to go on holding up the
Peter Plan, but because the alternative proposals would
not be accepted children would eventually suffer. The

Conservative Group could not honestly pursue such a policy. As a result representatives of the two sides met and agreed to recommend to the Education Committee that acceptance of the Peter Plan should be re-affirmed. This was done and confirmed later by the Council without dissent.

The long controversy was over.

3
Gateshead

The educational background

Few education authorities faced graver educational problems than Gateshead in the early 1950s. School buildings were old, an exceptional proportion of the children were in all-age schools, and the proportion of the 15-24 age group in full-time education was among the lowest in the country. The main limiting factor here was the unusually small ratio of selective secondary places. The town had only one grammar school. This problem was tackled first. A second grammar school was opened in 1956 and a third in 1961. A secondary technical school building followed in 1962, while the original grammar school moved into a new building the following year.

Meanwhile, Circular 342 of 1958 led to a successful drive to eliminate the all-age group. 40 per cent of Gateshead's children in the age-group 11-15 were still in such schools, while the national average was down to 11 per cent. A programme for seven new secondary modern schools was prepared and completed by 1965. The secondary school system was now as follows:

Selective schools	No. of places	Date of opening of building
Girls' Grammar	720	1956
Heathfield Grammar (co-ed)	720	1961
Elgin Secondary Tech. (co-ed)	650	1962
Boys' Grammar (re-housed)	720	1963
	2,810	

Non-selective (all secondary modern)		
Hill Head Boys'	450	1960
Hill Head Girls'	450	1960
Greenwell Boys'	600	1960
Greenwell Girls'	600	1963
Beacon Hill Boys'	600	1964
Beacon Hill Girls'	600	1964
Brackenbeds (co-ed)	600	1965
	3,900	

Two things are noteworthy about these figures. First, the predominance of single-sex over co-educational places: 4,740 as against 1,970. The significance of this will appear later. The second point is more immediately striking. Whereas, in 1967, 2,484 of 2,810 selective places were filled, only 2,224 of 3,900 non-selective places were taken up. The number of children in selective schools exceeded that in secondary moderns. This was partly because of the trend to stay on longer at school, partly because provision was made in building the secondary moderns for raising the school-leaving age to 16, and partly because Gateshead's falling population naturally leaves empty desks somewhere.

Primary school building proceeded more slowly. Nine new primary schools were opened between 1950 and 1966, but in proportion to the number of children involved a good deal remained to be done. When comprehensive education first became an issue in Gateshead, primary school teachers feared that their building programme might take second place to the adaptation of secondary schools to their new function. The education authority had to offer continual assurances to them throughout the comprehensive debate.

Gateshead's relationship with the diocesan Roman Catholic education authority was influential in the comprehensive scheme which emerged. Roman Catholics are numerous in Gateshead. The Vice-Chairman of the Education Committee (Councillor Harry Luxton) estimated that 'one-third of our children are Catholics'. This was something of an exaggeration. All Catholic children, however, do not attend Catholic schools, especially above primary level. There are three Roman Catholic secondary schools in Gateshead, namely:

St John Fisher (co-ed):   450 places: opened 1963;
St Aidan's (co-ed):   300 places: opened 1964;
St Wilfred's Secondary Modern:

      160 places: opened 1936.

The borough also assists many pupils who attend Roman Catholic grammar schools outside its boundaries.

The origin of the comprehensive scheme

Gateshead's successful school building programme left the authority with the problem that whatever comprehensive system was adopted, it would have to be based on the existing buildings. Yet Labour was in control throughout this period. Why, then, was it not carried through on comprehensive lines? The possibility was considered about the time when comprehensive education first became Labour policy at national level. 'The idea of comprehensive schooling was first discussed about 1957' (interview with Mr W. Coates). To explore the idea further, a Committee was set up in the following year with six members each from the Labour Party and the Labour Group on the Council. Two members of the Committee—Mr W. Coates and Alderman C. H. Wheatley—have played important parts in the development of the policy throughout. It considered material from Transport House, the N.U.T. and the National Foundation for Educational Research, as well as from a number of books. The Committee agreed on the principle of comprehension, but not on the particular pattern to be adopted in Gateshead. A suggested pilot scheme was defeated on the ground that it would be unjust to deny the possibility of selective places to children in one quarter only of the town.

Even had agreement been reached on how the comprehensive principle could be applied in Gateshead, there were difficulties in going ahead at that time. With a Conservative Government at Westminster, the introduction of a comprehensive scheme, while not impossible, would have been difficult. To fight, it was thought, would risk delaying the urgently needed school building programme. Locally, the grammar school teachers would probably have opposed comprehension even more vociferously in the 1950s than they did a decade later, since, with a Conservative Minister, they would have thought the chance of success higher. All in all, it was simpler for Gateshead to accept the existing pattern. The very success of the building programme seemed to make comprehensive schools less urgent, because of the exceptionally high proportion of selective places it provided. In the words of a Group discussion document, of two basic arguments for comprehensive education, '1. to increase flexibility between types of education, [and] 2. to do away with selection tests ... in Gateshead; the second only applies since 40 per cent of school-children enter grammar and technical secondary schools and transfer is normal'.

Given that the Labour Group was committed to comprehensive education but had to wait for more favourable circumstances to introduce it, why did they not prepare, under the building programme, for the switch to a comprehensive scheme? The structure which had been created by 1964 was not suitable for 11-18 schools, which are widely regarded as the best type, or even for the establishment of convenient links between junior and senior high schools. Alderman Wheatley claimed in interview that the secondary modern schools had been 'built with an eye to possible future conversion to comprehensive education'. But Mr Coates said that schools suitable for transformation into comprehensives catering for the 11-18 age-group *would* have been built 'but there was just not adequate acreage of building site'. It seems likely that there was no conscious policy decision to relate the building programme to a possible switch to comprehensive education. The need for speed militated against long-term planning.

If the comprehensive issue hung fire for some years, why did it come alive in 1964? First, the secondary building programme was virtually complete. The Education Committee, having accommodated the children, could now consider educational reorganization (interview with Mr Wheatley). Or, as Mr Coates put it: 'The secondary school system in the town had to be completed before the Committee could embark on a scheme of this [i.e. comprehensive] type' (*Gateshead Post*, 20 November, 1964). Second, the Director of Education (Mr Howard) was due to retire in November 1964 and his deputy (Mr Stokes), was appointed to succeed him. It is not asserted that one was an opponent, whilst the other was a champion, of the comprehensive idea, or that either usurped the policy-making role of the Education Committee. As Mr Howard's retirement was impending it would be very natural, too, for the Education Committee to prefer to launch a radical policy with a new man to see it through. Third, there was the General Election atmosphere of 1964, with the expectation that a Government favourable to comprehension would soon be in power.

In January 1964, the Chairman and Vice-Chairman of the Education Committee put forward 'preliminary proposals' to the Labour Group, and it was at this point that the basic principle of the future Gateshead system was laid down. There were to be junior and senior high schools based on the existing secondary modern and grammar schools. At this stage, Messrs Wheatley and Luxton were undecided as to the details of the scheme, except that a two-tier structure was required by the size and location of the new schools which had just been erected. During the last months of Mr Howard's reign, a certain amount of planning along similar lines was going on in his office and with his blessing. This paralleled discussions in the Group, and there were unofficial exchanges between politicians and administrators.

The Ministry's Circular 12/64 gave the opportunity to bring the question into the open. Its purpose was to explain the Education Act, 1964, which permitted the establishment of schools for children ranging in age from less than $10\frac{1}{2}$ to more than 12—that is, cutting out selection at eleven-plus. But its aim was narrow: 'to permit a relatively small number of limited experiments in educational organization .... [The Secretary of State] does not envisage using his powers to approve proposals designed to lead to the widespread recasting of the organization of maintained schools'. Nevertheless, in August 1964, the Schools Management Sub-Committee (S.M.S.-C.) requested its Chairman and Vice-Chairman, with the Deputy Director, to examine the possibility of secondary reorganization on the basis of the Circular (Minute 151). Their report reached the Education Committee in November 1964, (Minute 240). It contains the essentials of the scheme which was to emerge with ministerial approval in January 1967, and followed the main lines of the Leicestershire Plan:

1. Abandonment of the eleven-plus and all selection;

66

2. Transfer of all pupils at eleven-plus to junior high schools (J.H.S.);

3. Transfer of all pupils at fourteen-plus to senior high schools (S.H.S.).

Such wholesale reorganization went far beyond the bounds of the Circular. The programme was announced on the radio and in the Press. It was proclaimed as: 'A break for the eleven-plus failures ... revolutionary school plan for Gateshead ... drawn up by Ald. C. H. Wheatley, Chairman of the Education Committee, and the Vice-Chairman, Councillor Harry Luxton' (*Gateshead Post*, 20 November, 1964). It was dubbed the Luxton-Wheatley Plan.

In the same month (November 1964), a letter was sent by the Director of Education to all head teachers outlining the proposals, emphasizing the desire of the Education Committee for consultation, and requesting them to 'draw the attention of all members of your staff to this letter'. The immediate response of teachers came partly in the form of statements to the Education Committee by individual schools and groups of schools, and by the two main teachers' unions, and partly in the form of letters to the local press. At this time, there existed no institution through which teachers could express their views except their union organizations, principally the National Union of Teachers and the local Joint Four. But by March 1965, at the teachers' demand, there was also a Teachers' Joint Committee for Secondary Reorganization, with two working parties: one for selective school teachers and one for non-selective schools.

On the Council's side, the Schools Management Sub-Committee delegated seven of its members, who formed the General Purposes Committee (G.P.C.), to begin discussions with each of the teachers' bodies mentioned.

The standpoints of the different groups and the logic of the outcome might be best summarized as follows:

Type of organization The necessity of a two-tier system rather than an 11-18 age-group system was generally accepted from the outset, as a feature which was dictated by physical conditions, that is, the existing new school buildings. The Joint Four and the selective schools regretted this necessity and regarded it as an argument against the introduction of a comprehensive system on the grounds that any break in education, where a course has been embarked upon, was a bad thing.

Age of transfer The scheme was originally proposed to the Education Committee with 14+ as the age of transfer. The selective schools, however, argued that a 14+ break was particularly undesirable because it allowed only one year (at the maximum) in the S.H.S. for children who were leaving at 15. The Joint Four even submitted a plan demonstrating that it would be possible to make the break at 13+, if only those children who would stay at the S.H.S. beyond the school-leaving age were allowed to transfer from the J.H.Ss.

The Director argued that transfer at 13+ would be impractical since it would mean that only three J.H.Ss. would be feeding five S.H.Ss. if all children transferred. The system would be unbalanced: younger children would have to travel further to school, and some sort of arbitrary channelling device would have to be introduced to allocate children from a single J.H.S. to different S.H.Ss. Besides, there were only four schools already well enough equipped to be S.H.Ss. Even if optionality of transfer was accepted, the Joint Four's assumption of the continuance of present levels of leaving at age 15 was unrealistic. Ultimately, the age of transfer was settled on the ground that only 14+ was possible, given the existing school buildings.

Linkage There was no policy statement on linkage in the original proposals. This presented a special problem to members of the G.P.C. and the Director. On the one hand, linkage between specific J.H.Ss. and S.H.Ss. was seen to be a necessity, especially with a transfer age of 14+ when one year of the O level or C.S.E. course would already have been completed at the J.H.S. On the other hand, how could direct links between schools be established if parents were allowed to choose between co-educational and single-sex schools, and if numbers entering a S.H.S. from a particular J.H.S. might vary from year to year? On grounds of practicality, and the desirability of linkage, the Director therefore evolved a system of linkage between proposed J.H.Ss. and S.H.Ss. which assumed that all were *co-educational* and that *all children* transferred from the J.H.S. to the S.H.S.

Teachers of all types were agreed on the principle of the desirability of linkage if all children were to transfer at 14+ (of which the Joint Four did not approve). However, the selective schools stressed the difficulty of achieving this linkage, given the right of parents to choose between co-educational and single-sex schooling (quoting the 1944 Education Act). They recognized that effective linkage between specific schools would mean standardization on co-educational lines (unless the J.H.Ss. also were to be single-sex). Their attitude to linkage was therefore closely bound to their fight for single-sex education and for the limitation of transfer to the S.H.Ss. of those pupils who intended to stay beyond the school-leaving age. By thus cutting down on the numbers involved, they hoped (and attempted to prove that it would be possible) to preserve single-sex S.H.Ss. serving the town as a whole and not specific J.H.Ss.

Optionality of transfer After losing the battle for 13+ transfer, the selective schools thereafter fought for the transfer to S.H.Ss. from J.H.Ss. only of those children prepared to stay at school till the age of 16. The non-selective (secondary modern) schools working party declared itself in favour of total transfer, to avoid the duplication of courses between J.H.S. and S.H.S. and to ensure that all children would be given the fullest chance to be attracted to stay beyond the school-leaving age.

The Director came out strongly in favour of overall transfer at 14+. Administratively, this was necessary if there were to be linkage between schools. Also, staffing shortage would make it impossible to provide for O level or C.S.E. courses at both J.H.Ss. and S.H.Ss. (the Department of Education requires that pupils staying at J.H.Ss. up to school-leaving age should embark on G.C.E. courses); educationally, the Director's argument was that 'admission to senior schools should be regarded as an opening of new opportunities' which should be available to all children. A further point making total transfer conducive to administrative practicality was that, with the school-leaving age then expected to rise to 16 in 1970, and full transformation to comprehensive education expected only in 1970, the optional transfer system would only have one year's existence before it would require changing. Once the necessity for school linkage was accepted, total transfer seems to have followed inexorably.

Co-education The original proposals to the Schools Management Sub-Committee by Mr Luxton and Mr Wheatley made no mention of co-education. As has been shown, the new Director of Education (Mr Stokes), in producing plans for linking junior and senior schools, had discovered that this linkage was only possible if co-educational *or* single-sex education were assumed throughout. Single-sex education throughout, as the N.U.T. pointed out, would involve duplication of all staff, and by splitting schools into small units would render the provision of a 'comprehensive' range of courses impractical.

The three grammar schools and the Joint Four argued that the system should continue to offer the choice of co-education or single-sex schooling to parents. The

Rent and Ratepayers' Association supported them and added the argument that co-education would mean 'destroying the tradition' of the two single-sex grammar schools.

The non-selective schools' working party declared themselves 22 to 7 in favour of co-education, and were supported in this by the local N.U.T. With the Director of Education, the N.U.T. criticized the Joint Four scheme for a mixed system as impractical. Nor, they claimed, could it ensure the freedom of parents to exercise choice —parental choice would be limited by the number of places available in the surviving single-sex schools. According to Mr Wheatley, the Education Committee chairman, the retention of parental choice in this matter 'was not feasible'. Given the educational buildings existing, the ultimate decision on each of these issues was dictated by physical circumstances.

By March 1966, the Education Committee had decided in favour of a split system with the break at 14+ with co-education throughout, total transfer, and the linking of specific junior and senior high schools on a basis which allowed some flexibility for special cases. Eleven-plus selection was to end in 1968, and the new scheme was to be introduced in September of the same year.

The development of the scheme: roles of groups

This is a study of interest groups in the broadest sense. It is not a study merely of pressure groups acting from outside on the Council, but of all the interests within and outside it which, interacting, produce a decision. Within the legal framework of the Council, two bodies operate in the decision-making process, the administrative departments and the parties. In relation to the Council committees, the former exist formally on the basis of a co-operative division of functions—the committees formulating policy and the departments implementing it;

71

while the parties operate formally on the assumption of competition for the function of policy-making. The actual roles of the Education Office and the two parties in influencing the comprehensive scheme are discussed below.

The Education Office It has already been noted that there was considerable collaboration between the Education Office and key members of the Labour Group in the preparation of the draft proposals submitted to the Education Committee in November 1964. But the policy decision to 'go comprehensive' had been discussed (since 1958) and taken within the Group. It has also been seen that the responsibility for drawing up the briefs to the Labour Party, and later to the Education Committee, was delegated to Mr Stokes by Mr Howard (the Director) until his retirement in November 1964.

The opponents of the comprehensive plans seem to have assumed that both Directors were opposed to the scheme but forced to comply. A leading member of the local Joint Four thought that 'Mr Stokes got the job on the understanding that he would promote the scheme', as if this were something which would be naturally distasteful to Mr Stokes. There seems to be something in this of an attempt to explain their own weakness in terms of the 'tyranny' of the Labour Party over neutral 'good sense'. A later statement by the same Joint Four member seems to be more realistic : 'Whatever his personal views, he [Mr Stokes] sees himself as a servant of the Committee, as a professional person.'

The early collaboration of the Labour Group and Mr Stokes developed further after the Schools Management Sub-Committee had heard the proposals and referred them to the General Purposes Committee for consideration. On the G.P.C., out of seven members there was only one Rent and Ratepayer, and Mr Stokes was merely putting the view of the majority of the Committee in defending

72

the draft proposals against the criticism of the Joint Four and the selective schools, and in developing a scheme on the basis of the two November propositions that there should be transfer at 14+ and that all children should go on to S.H.Ss. It was in the interests of both the G.P.C. and the Director that the most practical scheme should be introduced, on the basis of these propositions, a theme which recognized the physical limitations imposed by the existing building structure. On the Director fell the responsibility of drafting papers for the consideration of the General Purposes Committee, and of presenting the case of the G.P.C. to the Teachers' Joint Committee and the teachers' unions. Mr Stokes said in interview: 'They [the Education Committee] pinned their faith on me.'

The Director's role at this stage was central. He outlined the draft proposals to a special meeting of teachers held in January 1965, and received the written communications of the teachers' unions and working parties which came in response to his invitation for comments on the scheme. The G.P.C. was made aware of the problems which arose in the formulating of the plans, but it was for the Director to propose solutions, and in December 1965, he presented to the Committee a scheme of linked schools based on standardized co-education as the only means by which it could be effectively achieved. This scheme, after consideration by the G.P.C. was proposed to the Teachers' Joint Committee by Mr Luxton (the Vice-Chairman of the G.P.C.) as a motion and adopted by a majority vote.

It is possible to argue that at the stage of evolving an administratively practicable scheme, the Director was predominant over the Chairman and Vice-Chairman of the Education Committee; but the predominance seems to have been technical, and untested by any real clash of interests. For example, neither the Chairman nor the Vice-Chairman appear to have considered the necessity of the linking of specific schools or the co-education throughout the system which followed from it, before the Director posed the problem and produced the solutions. To the Labour Group, these were technical points on which any decision was a good one if it allowed the early introduction of a comprehensive scheme. Especially after the receipt of Circular 10/65 in July 1965, from the Department of Education and Science, requesting the submission of plans for re-organization, the interest of politicians and their chief administrator alike was in the formulation of a scheme without delay for submission by August 1966.

The parties The Labour Party's long period of control of the borough has had repercussions on its internal structure. Dominant figures within the Group in Council tend to be long-established in their offices and from this position of strength to dominate the borough Party. The key office-holders in the borough Party are also important members of the Council. This, combined with the fact that except for monthly meetings of the General Management Committee, Party members only meet at ward level, severely reduced the possibility of members of the Party who are not councillors having any effect on policy matters. There is a Joint Policy Committee of the Group and town Party, but (as has been stated) these two bodies are in any case dominated by the same people, and policy-making in fact appears to rest with the Group Policy Committee which has three members of the town Party co-opted in a consultative capacity.

The Group Policy Committee meets monthly before full Council meetings to decide whether to endorse or refer back points in the various committees' minutes, but there are no separate meetings of Labour Party members of specific Council committees. This again appears to indicate a centralization of decision-making, even within the Group.

74

The Party in Gateshead, then, is centralized as well as firmly established in power. This gives an inevitability to its policy decisions—there is little chance of a challenge to a policy decision emerging from within the Party or from the opposition Party. This inevitability supports the formal division of functions: the Director of Education accepts the policy decision and the Party trusts him to implement it, allowing him to develop it into an administratively workable scheme.

The length of tenure of office by the Labour Party and its councillors also makes for close relations with the Council departments: by 1967, Mr Wheatley had been Chairman of the Education Committee for nine years and Vice-Chairman before that; Mr Luxton had been vice-Chairman for five years; Mr Coates had been a co-opted member of the Committee for 17 years, and Mr Stokes had been Deputy Director, or Director, as long as any of these had held office.

The Rent and Ratepayers' Group was in a correspondingly weak position. The Association was founded in 1920, and until after the war did not play any direct role in local politics, limiting its activities to the support of the 'moderates' on the Council. Since the war, it has acted locally as a political party but has never held power in Gateshead. Its representation in a Council of 48 (including 12 aldermen) was 8 in 1967.

Without the promise of a councillorship, as reward for services to the Association, and without safe seats for any but a few of the Rent and Ratepayers' leaders, the Party has not been able to maintain the continuity of command which characterizes the Labour Party; nor, for the same reasons, has its group in Council attained the same predominance over the outside Party as is the case with the Labour Party. For example, the Chairman of the Association lost his seat as a councillor in 1966 and the Rent and Ratepayers were unable even to gain him a place as a co-opted member of the Education Committee.

The Rent and Ratepayers' Association is, anyway, much more loosely structured than the Labour Party. Constitutionally, its members and councillors are 'free to vote as they like on Council matters, except that they are pledged to economy'. This could take in any shade of political opinion, but in fact members state that they are united by a common 'anti-socialist' stance which, in this case, means opposition to the dominant Labour Party. A monthly Group meeting is held but, according to Rent and Ratepayer informants, member councillors are not bound by this to any party line.

Most obviously, the weakness of the Rent and Ratepayers on the comprehensive issue stemmed from their low representation. Throughout the period of debate on comprehensive education they had three representatives on the Education (and hence the Schools Management) Committee. On the General Purposes Committee, to which the matter was referred, their representation was down to one.

The weakness of the Rent and Ratepayers' position made it possible for the Director to co-operate fully with the Labour Group in the elaboration of draft proposals, confident in the knowledge that he was dealing with the Group which would remain in power for the foreseeable future. This allowed proposals to be developed to an advanced stage before the Rent and Ratepayers' Group was able to consider them. According to Mr Rogers (a Rent and Ratepayer councillor) the plans were presented to the Committee in November 1964, in detail, 'as a sort of *fait accompli*', without there having been any previous call by the Committee for a report on comprehensive education.

That the Rent and Ratepayers did respond to the proposals in the same Committee meeting, in spite of the lack of any foreknowledge or party line on comprehensives, seems to have been due to Mr Rogers, to whom 'all comprehensive systems are poison'.

Within the Schools Management Sub-committee, to which the proposals were presented in November 1964, Mr Rogers's aim appears to have been to win the initiative from the Labour Group by putting them back on the defensive. He responded to the proposals in the same meeting by tabling a motion:

> That this Committee reaffirms its confidence in its existing and newly reorganized system of secondary schools: and hereby determines to give the system ten years in which to operate before undertaking any major review of the Borough's arrangements for secondary education (*Gateshead Post*, 20 November, 1964).

In an interview, Mr Rogers declared that his main objective was to force the Labour councillors to admit no-confidence in the system which they had created, as a basis for a further attack on them.

The Chairman (Mr Wheatley) attempted to overcome the threat by reducing the motion to an amendment in the following meeting of the Education Committee: 'It was common practice,' said Ald. Wheatley, 'to treat it as an amendment' (*Gateshead Post*, 27 November, 1964). This would deny Mr Rogers the opportunity of speaking for the motion and the right of reply; that is, the opportunity of publicizing the comprehensive scheme (Committee meetings are reported in the local Press). The Chairman claimed in the Committee that the Town Clerk had advised him that the treating of this motion as an amendment was justifiable. In fact, he had *not* consulted the Town Clerk; instead, his Vice-Chairman had gained some sort of assurance on the matter from an official of the Town Clerk's Department and communicated it to him. The Chairman was forced to make an apology before the full Council to the Town Clerk for attributing to him an improper interpretation of Standing Orders.

The end result was that Mr Rogers, who fully exploited

this further embarrassment of the Labour Group, gained more publicity than he would have done out of the motion itself (the amendment was defeated by 25 to 3 votes, but was reported in the minutes as a motion). Three letters from Mr Rogers on the motion, and the attempt to quash it, were published in the *Gateshead Post*, and the newspaper also carried two reports on the events in the Council chamber. The use by the Rent and Ratepayers of the local Press was fully recognized by Mr Wheatley: 'Ald. Wheatley said he had been criticized publicly by Coun. Rogers with regard to the matter, but this he treated with the contempt it deserved.' Alderman Wheatley said of Councillor Rogers: 'You fly to the Press before approaching anyone else' (*Gateshead Post*, 11 November, 1964).

Before the matter was finally referred to the G.P.C., of which he was not a member, Mr Rogers prevented its leaving the full Education Committee in a form which would have strengthened the position of the G.P.C. in its negotiations with teachers' bodies. He reported in the *Gateshead Post* (8 January, 1965) that in 'the Education Committee meeting on November 23 last ... the strange resolution appear[ed] in the minutes of the Schools Management Sub-Committee (meeting on November 13) stating that the Sub-Committee recommended approval "in principle" of the proposals'. In fact this recommendation, he reported, had never been made, and (Mr Rogers goes on): 'Then the Mayor got up and agreed that the printed resolution was an "error" and the Committee consented merely to "note" the proposals—a very different matter from approving them "in principle".'

Recognizing the weakness of the Rent and Ratepayers in the Council, Mr Rogers seems to have aimed at publicizing the scheme and bringing the discussion into the open. After the Committee meeting at which the proposals were presented he contacted Mr Fawcett of the Joint Four and informed him of the development, and wrote to the local newspaper with a long criticism of the proposals and defence of the existing system. His object was to raise an informed opposition outside the Council (in which the Rent and Ratepayers were ineffectual) among 'parents, teachers, pupils, and all interested in the education of Gateshead's children'. Opening one letter (*Gateshead Post*, 20 November, 1964) with: 'The people of Gateshead should realize what is at stake', he proceeded to outline the proposals and his objections. His letter claimed that children at no level of ability would benefit by the scheme, and that the proposed change would create 'havoc for both pupils and teachers' treating them 'as mere cattle to be moved from one byre to another'. In other words, everybody had a reason for protesting against the proposals.

But much of Mr Rogers's attack was not on the principle of comprehensive education but on the 'politics' of its introduction in Gateshead: (1) The power of the 'local Labour Party machine backed by a Labour Government' to push an unpopular decision through. (2) The lack of preliminary consultations with teachers—'Why? I suspect that the answer is POLITICAL not education.' (3) The assumption of the Chairman and Vice-Chairman that their proposals 'were definitely to be implemented'. (4) The partiality of a system where the Chairman and Vice-Chairman of the Education Committee were also those of the General Purposes Committee which sits 'in judgment on other viewpoints' (*Gateshead Post*, 20 November, 1964).

These last four points were to be taken up by the Joint Four secretary. But the forceful opposition of the Rent and Ratepayers was short-lived. This was for three reasons (apart from factors contributing to their weaknesses already mentioned): (1) the reference of the matter to the G.P.C. where the Rent and Ratepayers had only one representative (who was not Mr Rogers). (2) Mr Rogers's opposition to the principle of comprehension which made negotiation over details irrelevant to him. (3) The retirement of Mr Rogers from the Council in May 1965.

With the emergence of Teacher-G.P.C. 'bargaining machinery' the Rent and Ratepayer councillors acted mainly by supporting the Joint Four in the argument against the plans as 'make-shift' and 'a rushed job'. They had been too weak to be influential within the Council Chamber.

Only two main categories of outside organizations appear to have had any relations with the Gateshead Council over the issue of comprehensive education: teachers' bodies, and the Roman Catholic education authorities.

Teachers' organizations At the time that the issue of comprehensive education came up in Gateshead, there were seven teachers' associations represented in the borough: The National Union of Teachers, The National Association of Schoolmasters, The National Association of Head Teachers, The Association of Headmasters, The Association of Headmistresses, The Assistant Masters' Association, The Assistant Mistresses' Association. In the debate, these broke down into two main groups: the Gateshead Teachers' Association of The National Union of Teachers, and the Joint Four (consisting of the last four associations).

Besides these already existing organizations, there was one set up to act as a purely local representative organization—The Teachers' Joint Committee for Secondary Reorganization. This consisted of two representatives from each of the secondary schools, eight representatives of the primary schools, two Roman Catholic school representatives, and the secretaries of the seven teachers' organizations as observers. It was broken down into two working parties for the representation of interests to the G.P.C.—the selective (or grammar and secondary technical) schools' and the non-selective (or secondary modern) schools' working parties. In practice, in membership and

80

policy lines, the non-selective schools' working party and the N.U.T. formed one grouping, and the selective schools' working party and the local Joint Four another.

The relations which already existed between teachers' organizations and the Council, when the comprehensive system became an issue, were weighted heavily in favour of the non-selective schools and the N.U.T. The N.U.T. is by far the largest single teachers' organization in Gateshead. For this reason it dominated the Joint Consultative Committee which existed before the comprehensive issue ever emerged. This was an organization linking the teachers and the Education Committee, teachers being elected to it as representatives. Since they were elected by majority vote, no other teachers' association but the N.U.T. was represented on it. Another institutionalized connection between the teachers and the Council was the member co-opted to the Education Committee to represent the teachers. Since 1950, another co-opted seat had been occupied by a member of the N.U.T., Mr Coates. Through him, the local Labour Party and the local N.U.T. had strong personal connections— he was both the president of the N.U.T. and the treasurer of the Labour Party, as well as co-opted member of the Education Committee.

These contacts and its large membership put the N.U.T. in a particularly powerful position in the framing of educational policy. It had access to policy discussions and the formulation of plans within both the Labour Group and the Education Committee. In order to gain representation on the Joint Consultative Committee, 'the preserve of the N.U.T.', four of the other teachers' associations formed the grouping of the Joint Four. This was in summer 1964, so that at the beginning of the negotiations the local Joint Four was still new, with only the rudiments of organization. Neither did it, until some time after, achieve representation on the Joint Consultative machinery.

As the N.U.T. had contacts with the Labour Party, the Joint Four had contacts with the Rent and Ratepayers' Association, even before they were united by the comprehensive issue. Mr Rogers was an ex-pupil of Mr Fawcett (the Secretary of the Joint Four) and they had continued their relationship. This was to be of little use to the Joint Four, however, due to the Rent and Ratepayers' own weakness, except that much of the Joint Four's initial information on the scheme came from Mr Rogers.

If these were their power positions, how far were the teachers' groupings able to use them to influence the comprehensive plans?

From the first announcement of the draft proposals, the Chairman and Vice-Chairman of the Education Committee committed themselves to: 'fullest consultation with parents and teachers ... before any proposals are published.' This was supported by the Director of Education in his letter to teachers outlining the proposals and promising 'the closest consultation' (November 1964). But the Joint Four and the Labour Group had different views of the purpose of consultations. The one wished to question the principle of comprehension, the other to discuss its implementation.

For the Joint Four, as Mr Fawcett stated in the press: 'Parents and teachers have the right to consultation, not only on reorganization but also on its necessity and desirability' (*Gateshead Post*, 18 December, 1964). For the Education Committee on the other hand, as Mr Wheatley stated in interview: 'The idea was to gain the co-operation of the teachers because the success of the scheme depends on them.' Or, as the draft proposals by Mr Wheatley and Mr Luxton stated more bluntly: 'The scheme needs to be "sold" to (a) the public, (b) teaching staffs.' The view of the Labour Group was in close accord with the statement in Circular 10/65: 'the Secretary of State believes that once the principles and main outlines of a possible plan or reorganization have been formulated, *there should follow* a period of close and genuine consultation with teachers' (our italics).

Until about June 1965, when the Teachers' Joint Committee began to function, the Joint Four (led by Mr Fawcett) and individual grammar school staffs took a stand wholly hostile to the scheme, urging the retention of the existing system: 'The present proposals, however feasible administratively, are, on educational grounds, completely unacceptable' (letter from Joint Four to Education Committee, 3 February, 1965).

Mr Fawcett wrote regular and critical letters to the Press through the period until June 1965. His case was that while he admitted that it was 'the prerogative of the elected representatives' to make the policy decision, the chance should, at some stage, have been given to the teachers to advise the policy-makers: 'my main concern has always been to deplore the complete lack of all consultation *prior* to the announcement of a scheme' (*Gateshead Post*, 29 January, 1965). 'There is a feeling that if consultation is offered now, this is simply because without it ministerial approval for the scheme would not be forthcoming' (*Gateshead Post*, 18 December, 1964). The Committee chairman's reply to this charge was that proposals had to be provided 'as a start for the debate', and that, 'it is up to the local authority to decide the policy'. In a county borough with a more balanced party system, the policy decision would probably have been discussed more fully in the Council. An opposition group would probably at this stage have consulted the Joint Four, allowing it some involvement in policy-making. Specific proposals would not have emerged with majority Council backing at such an early stage and with such little warning. As it was, the Joint Four were thrown back into the reactive role shared by the Rent and Ratepayers: 'At the beginning, all we could do was to make destructive criticism since we had not had time to formulate counter-proposals' (interview with Mr Fawcett).

Since the Council had not acted as a forum, for the discussion of policy, and since no special bargaining machinery was set up until March 1965, (and then not consulted by the Education Committee until June) the Joint Four, like the Rent and Ratepayers, were left with only the local Press as a public forum.

In March 1965, the Teachers' Joint Committee was formed, after being proposed by the teachers' bodies. The function of this new machinery was interpreted differently by the Council and the Joint Four, in accordance with their different view of the purpose of consultations, and this increased hostility on both sides. Mr Fawcett (who resigned his grammar school teacher's post in June 1965), as secretary of the Joint Four, maintained his argument that after the 'widespread publication of the plan', any consultations 'could only be nominal'. By July, however, at the request of the Director, the two working parties had submitted their comments on the scheme.

The selective schools' working party note to the Education Committee (1 June, 1965) was more conciliatory than the Joint Four had been, accepting as its terms of reference the scheme as proposed by the Education Committee. It continued to attack the Education Committee's proposals, but also offered counter-proposals for a thirteen-plus transfer and a mixed co-education and single-sex system. None of these proposals was accepted and, in January 1967, the local Joint Four attempted a final line of resistance by appealing to their national organization to express their opinion of the scheme to the Secretary of State for Education. This move was ineffective, and was probably only intended as a demonstration of continued resistance.

The non-selective schools and the N.U.T. at no time made any comment in the Press. Their first recorded statements (in July 1965), accepted the Council's scheme in principle; their appeal was for the improvement of teachers' conditions (staff : student ratios, in-service training, future reservation of responsible appointments to local teachers). Otherwise, their commitment to the principle of comprehensive education coincided with that of the Labour Party, and their views on specific aspects of the scheme coincided with what the Director found to be administratively practicable solutions. There was no reason why they should attempt to exert their influence outside the formal consultative machinery, and their informal contacts with the Labour Party and the Education Committee.

The influence of teachers' opinions where they were in opposition to those of the Director and the Education Committee seems to have been negligible. In interview, the Director stated emphatically that the plan suffered no important changes from its inception to its final approval by the Education Committee—that is, no changes resulting from the influence of outside bodies.

The local Joint Four and the selective schools' working party claimed not to be against comprehensive education in principle, but against the scheme proposed. But many grammar school teachers were neither against the principle of comprehension nor willing to fight against the proposed scheme. Teachers interviewed felt that, generally, younger grammar school teachers tended to be less opposed to the scheme than the older ones, though they did fear being assigned to a J.H.S.; the older grammar school teachers probably had their opposition moderated by the fact that they were relatively secure in their positions at the head of the schools and unlikely to wish to prejudice them. As a potential interest group, the grammar school teachers were also in the compromising position of being employed by the agency on which they might wish to exert pressure.

This weak position of the Joint Four, even over its own membership, was demonstrated in June 1965. Mr Fawcett warned in the *Gateshead Post* of large-scale resignations among grammar school teachers if the 'plan goes through in the form proposed'. He resigned and claimed that at least twenty others had also done so: 'In my 21 years' service at the Boys' Grammar School the present number of staff leaving, coupled with the number prepared to leave, is quite unprecedented' (*Gateshead Post*, 2 July, 1965). The danger did not materialize, however. There were sixteen resignations from Gateshead selective secondary schools in 1965, as against an annual average of seven over the period 1957-1964—appreciably higher, but nothing approaching a mass exodus.

The Roman Catholics The Roman Catholic Education authority, unlike the grammar school teachers, represented an interest group with the potential of effective resistance. Their co-operation was not only desirable but necessary to the Council, which had no direct control over the section of the school provision managed by the Catholics.

The necessity was recognized by the Labour Group and Director, both in the draft proposals—'Regard must be given to the voluntary schools'—and in a Press statement by Mr Luxton: 'separate consultations will be held with the Roman Catholic Schools to make sure their special problems are satisfactorily resolved' (*Newcastle Journal*, 17 November, 1964).

The Roman Catholic schools in Gateshead are administered by the Diocesan Education Council (under the Bishop of Hexham and Newcastle), which is responsible to the National Catholic Education Council. They therefore stand in a largely autonomous position to the Council, though they are ultimately dependent on government support. The Council, with about one-sixth of Gateshead's children attending Roman Catholic schools, was concerned to achieve an agreement with the Diocesan Authorities which would allow the close integration of the state and voluntary system.

The Council and the Roman Catholic authorities therefore stand in mutual need of co-operation—especially where, as in Gateshead, the Council's policy is in accord with that of the government on whose funds the Roman Catholics depend for buildings and teachers' salaries. This mutual need is supported by policy statements from both sides. Archbishop Beck, chairman of the Catholic Education Council, wrote: 'In the first place, it is obviously desirable for the voluntary schools and the county schools in a given area to follow the same pattern.' The government Circular 10/65 of July 1965, also stated the need for co-operation: 'the plans which the Secretary of State is now requesting authorities to prepare should embrace' voluntary schools. Authorities should open discussions 'where appropriate with diocesan authorities, with a view to reaching agreement on how these schools can best be re-organized on comprehensive lines'.

The structure for the achievement of this co-operation already existed in Gateshead in the shape of an inter-parochial committee which, according to Mr Coates, was set up in 1948 with the express purpose of providing means of co-ordination with local and state authorities over a broad range of issues. Its effective leaders were a local priest and, on educational matters especially, Mr Coates, whose central role in the evolution of the comprehensive scheme has already been illustrated. As well as his other positions, he is also a Roman Catholic secondary school headmaster. With Mr Coates as co-ordinator, there could be little chance that the inter-parochial committee would oppose the Council's scheme.

The Roman Catholic authorities made no statement in the Press and hardly entered into the discussions between the G.P.C. and the Teachers' Joint Committee, though they were represented on the latter. Negotiations with the Catholics were conducted in a less formalized manner. 'Through Mr Coates we got the Roman Catholics acquainted with our ideas,' stated Mr Wheatley, and they evolved their own scheme in the knowledge of that of the Council. At an appropriate stage, the Director called a meeting in his office of all Roman Catholic parish priests and explained to them the Education Committee's plans with regard to the council schools. The effect of these upon the Roman Catholic schools was discussed. Contact was maintained between Mr Stokes and the priest referred to in the previous paragraph. In addition, Mr Coates acted as a 'very important link' (Mr Wheatley), 'a contact between the powers that be (Mr Coates), using the existing institution, the inter-parochial committee.

All discussion on the features of possible comprehensive schemes took place not between the Council and the Roman Catholic authorities, but within the Roman Catholic camp. According to Mr Coates, he explained the plans of the Education Committee to the Diocesan Education Council and was able to persuade them to adopt a system which would be compatible with that of the borough. 'We had a few differences with the Bishop, but [only] on points of detail'; the Bishop wanted 'transfer at 13-plus but we resisted that'. A meeting between the Roman Catholic teachers and the Bishop seems to have impressed on the latter that the teachers supported 14-plus transfer. One of the arguments used by the teachers was that with smaller J.H.Ss. (if the leaving age was 13), the grant from the government for graded teaching posts would be reduced.

In December 1965, the Director was able to report to the Education Committee that the Roman Catholics had indicated their wish to join the scheme. But it was not until June 1966, that he was able to report their plans to the Committee. That their plans were ready by the Department of Education and Science's August 1966, deadline, seems to have owed a good deal to pressure applied to the Catholic authorities by the Director through Mr Coates and the priest referred to above. Possibly, the Catholics did not treat the matter with the same urgency as the Council, but they were faced with the problem of devising a scheme which would blend with the schemes of other local authorities within the diocese, and which would also function as a unified system.

The scheme that was eventually submitted to the Education Committee in June 1966, and approved, depended on the Committee's support in the building of a new school in Blaydon, County Durham. Until this school was built, and other local authorities in the South Tyneside area had helped in the construction and adaptation of other new schools, the Roman Catholic schools would retain the selection procedure in some districts.

In contrast to the case of the Joint Four, the Council's contacts with the Roman Catholics were made through existing channels of communication. The two bodies stood in mutual need of co-operation and on this basis were united in their use of the channels to arrive at a solution acceptable to both sides.

The parents   Parents represent a body from which interest groups may be expected to emerge. In some local authority areas, such as Bristol, parents' organizations have been active in opposing the 'destruction' of grammar schools. Yet, in Gateshead there was no group attempt either to use any existing channels of communication (as the Catholics did), or to demand the creation of new consultative machinery (as the teachers did) to make parental views known to the authority.

The parents in Gateshead had no existing institution of communication with either teachers or the Council: the only Parent-Teacher Association functioning in the borough was created in December 1966: there were no associations of ex-pupils. Nor did any consultative machinery come into existence during the period; neither in the form of a committee similar to that of the teachers, nor even in the loose form of public meetings.

The draft proposals of November 1964, showed an awareness of the potential public reaction to the comprehensive scheme. There was thought to be a need not

89

only that the scheme should be '"sold" to the public', but also that there should be 'fullest consultation with parents ... '. The term 'senior high grammar school' was proposed for the senior high schools, 'as it might help combat opposition to elimination of grammar schools which is not necessarily Party policy'. It appears to have been believed that there was a real threat of opposition to the scheme from grammar school parents. But the drafters of the proposals were not only concerned with public reaction; they also saw it as a duty of the Council to provide education in accordance with the wishes of parents as laid down in s.76 of the 1944 Education Act. Therefore, 'some reliable indication of parental wishes would appear to be a prerequisite to any future useful consideration of this matter' (draft Proposals).

The similarity of the promise to teachers and parents was not confirmed in practice. Both, at this stage, were regarded as groups with which co-operation would be necessary if the scheme was to be smoothly implemented. But the teachers already had associations through which they could form their opinions and demand consultative machinery. The parents had none, and no group opinion emerged in reaction to the proposals. It is suggested that this allowed the Council to omit setting up machinery through which to inform parents and hear their views.

The promise of consultation with, and information of, parents was never entirely dropped by the Education Committee in its own, and its members', public statements. The government Circular 10/65 in July 1965, reinforced their commitment at least to inform, if not to consult with, parents:

> Parents cannot be consulted in the same way as teachers, but it is important that they should be informed fully and authoritatively as soon as practicable in the planning stage. Explanations by elected members and officers can be given at meetings, in schools, in booklets and through the Press.

In a letter to the Press (*Gateshead Post*, 23 July, 1965), the chairman, Mr Wheatley, reaffirmed the Committee's intention to inform *and* consult with parents. Mr Luxton, the Vice-Chairman, in a statement to the Press published two days earlier (*Newcastle Journal*, 21 July, 1965), went further and claimed that consultations with parents were already under way: 'Now, negotiations are going on between teachers, parents and all who are concerned.'

A year later (in July 1966), there had still been no public meetings nor any other attempt by the Council to publicize the change to comprehensive education, though the Education Committee had four months earlier, in March 1966, approved the scheme. In July, the Director was requested by the Committee to make arrangements to prepare draft publicity material for general issue to the public. The following February, 1967, the Schools Management Sub-Committee recommended the issue of the Director's explanatory booklet and its distribution to the parents, following the Secretary of State's approval of Gateshead's scheme at the end of January.

The booklet was issued to parents ten months later, in December 1967. Until then, the only publicly available means by which parents had been able to inform themselves were newspaper reports, Education Committee minutes, 'speech day' references to the scheme by Council members, and (on request) information from individual teachers and councillors.

But would consultation with parents have been feasible? Mr Stokes, the Director, was sure that it would not: teachers could not have been consulted without a plan as a basis for consultation; and parents could not be informed without a plan as a basis for information. There was no value in consulting parents whose views would be uninformed, 'limited and subjective'; and if parents were to be informed, it could only be after the plan was fully approved by the Department of Education. Besides, he guessed from the 'extraordinary little reaction from parents' that most of them approved of the scheme.

According to one member of the Labour Group, the Chairman of the Committee claimed justification for the dropping of the idea of parental consultation in Circular 10/65. According to this document, parents could not be consulted in the same way as teachers. But it stressed that they should be informed 'as soon as practicable in the planning stage'.

The argument of those responsible for not deliberately informing parents was, therefore, that information could not usefully be passed on to parents until a comprehensive plan was approved by the Secretary of State. But even after this approval, in January 1967, parents were not informed.

The view that consultation was impracticable, and even undesirable in principle, was not accepted without argument within the Labour Group. Mr Coates claimed that he pressed for consultations with parents: 'I wanted meetings in every ward, or, failing that, at least four meetings in the town.' According to him, it was not so much any deliberate opposition in principle to these meetings as an unwillingness to hinder the development of final plans. 'Plans had to be submitted by 1 August, 1966, and by June we were in a hurry to get through teachers' consultations.' The Circular 10/65 provided an escape from the commitment to consultation. Mr Coates claimed that Roman Catholic parents, by contrast, had been fully informed through church announcements and parochial meetings throughout the period that comprehensive education was being discussed.

It seems that the Council was loath to risk exciting a public interest which might impede the progress of the scheme. It is difficult to see at what point, in this case, the general public could have become informed enough to react to the proposals. On the one hand, they were regarded as not sufficiently informed to be consulted, and lack of public response was taken to imply indifference or tacit approval; on the other, it was felt that no information could be supplied until the plan was approved, which effectively excluded the possibility of consultation.

That there was slight public response to the plans is easily seen. The Education Office received no communications from parents. The teachers interviewed agreed that few parents had made enquiries to them about the scheme. One case appears in the Education Committee minutes of a request from a public group for information on the scheme. This came from a Youth and Community Centre and asked for a talk on the comprehensive scheme. There was no mention in the minutes of this having been followed up, and, indeed, on investigation it emerged that the Community Centre committee had forgotten that they had ever made the request, and no speaker had visited them.

The Press comment was probably the most publicly available means by which parents could inform themselves. From the vigorous criticism of the scheme by Mr Rogers and Mr Fawcett in the *Gateshead Post*, it might have been expected that some response would have been drawn from the public. That there was none is a measure of the failure of the Rent and Ratepayers and the Joint Four to gain support for their opinions by bringing the debate into the open. As Mr Coates said, the correspondence in the *Gateshead Post* 'at least had the merit that it publicized the facts', but 'this was a poor substitute' for public meetings.

Ministerial approval

The plan was put into its final shape, and approved by the authority, in the spring of 1966. Two additional features had been added to the original scheme:

—each J.H.S. was to be linked to a specific S.H.S.: deviation from this pattern would be permitted only in special circumstances, e.g., when the number to be transferred exceeded the places available;—parents would have no choice between single-sex and co-educational schools.

In June 1966, the Secretary of State approved the scheme in principle, reserving a final decision until the plans of neighbouring authorities had been received. Difficulty arose in September 1966, over the cost of adapting school buildings to meet their new needs. The Department of Education and Science thought the authority's estimates too high, and a deputation in December 1966, failed to get a favourable verdict. However, the aid of the borough's two M.P.s (both Labour) was invoked and they seem to have achieved at least a measure of success (*Gateshead Post*, 3 February, 1967). At last, ministerial approval was given in January 1967, with sanction for building to the value of £100,000 as compared with the authority's request for a programme costing £160,000.

4
Conclusion

The contrasts between the two towns are obvious, but
not in all cases those that might be expected. The competitive politics of Darlington might be supposed to put
a premium on party solidarity. Yet the hardest fight there
for the comprehensive principle was within the Labour
Party itself. In the Gateshead Labour Party, on the other
hand, which could have much better afforded the luxury
of a split, no evidence of any difference of view emerged.
In consequence, the Gateshead story can be told with
scarcely any reference to the Council outside the Education Committee. The majority on the former was prepared to endorse the proposals of the latter as sound
Party policy. In Darlington, on the other hand, the pro-
comprehensive faction used the Party Group, the General
Purposes Committee and the Council itself in its struggle
against its opponents within the Labour Party.

Similarly, it might have been expected that the necessity to fight for every vote in Darlington would stimulate
hard thinking about policy. In fact, Labour's attitude to
comprehensive schools suggests that leading members of
the Party were satisfied with very broad policy gestures,
leaving it to the Chief Education Officer to work out the
details. In Gateshead, on the other hand, where Labour's
long and secure tenure of power might have induced a
somnolent attitude towards policy, members of the Educa-

tion Committee put real effort into working out a comprehensive policy in a fair degree of detail. They worked in partnership with their Director of Education, of course, but without delegating all the work to him. It seems symbolically fitting that the Gateshead plan was known by the name of two members of the Council, whereas in Darlington the scheme went under the name of the Chief Education Officer.

The Gateshead case throws light on the concepts of policy and administration, which are imperfectly understood by many otherwise well-informed people. Two fallacies are very widespread. One is that the administrator is a Machiavellian grey eminence, manipulating his political masters like puppets. The other would reduce the role of the administrator to that of a mere clerk, carrying out policy in a mechanical and routine fashion. In fact, of course, politician and administrator work in partnership. The Gateshead case-study provides a good example of this. The Luxton-Wheatley plan left open two important options: whether children leaving the J.H.S. should have any choice among the S.H.Ss.: and whether there should be any choice at secondary level between single-sex and co-educational schools. The Director, in working out the implications of the Luxton-Wheatley principles, showed that they would operate most effectively if there were very close links between each J.H.S. and a single S.H.S. and if co-education became the rule throughout the secondary school system. The Education Committee, guided by his advice, incorporated these additional points in the plan. The new attitude towards co-education marks a most striking departure from the authority's previous practice. As shown above, single-sex places out-numbered co-educational places by roughly two to one in Gateshead secondary schools. The linkage between J.H.Ss. and S.H.Ss. will set strict limits to the future development of education in the borough. Since each of the latter will have to provide a full range of the basic subjects, the

96

scope for each to develop a distinct line of its own will be correspondingly reduced. In their consequences for future generations of Gateshead children, the aspects the plan adopted on the recommendation of the Director will prove not less important than those which originated with members of the Education Committee. The relationship between politician and administrator in the formation of policy was a partnership. The administrator did not merely carry out precepts inscribed on tablets handed down from a high place.

It might appear that the Gateshead authority rode roughshod over the reasoned case for amendment made out by their main critics, the grammar school teachers. The eventual scheme could be represented as the off-spring of the Gateshead Labour Party and the Gateshead N.U.T. It would be nearer the mark to say that it is by architecture out of geography. Gateshead is bisected by the A1 at its unmotorwayed worst. Any borough administrator has, therefore, to keep down to the minimum traffic across this highway. The secondary school system has in consequence been reorganized as two sub-systems, as far as possible independent of each other. Moreover, reorganization did not begin until the secondary school building programme was substantially complete. When Circular 10/65 appeared, not one of Gateshead's secondary schools was more than ten years old. Clearly, there was no prospect of getting permission to erect even one purpose-built comprehensive. Whatever system was adopted had to be based on the existing buildings. The pattern of J.H.Ss. and S.H.Ss. seemed to be the best in the circumstances, and the size of the premises determined that the break should be at fourteen-plus rather than thirteen-plus. With the twin advantages of hindsight and irresponsibility, it would be easy for a critic to condemn the authority for putting the cart before the horse. It could forcefully be argued that they should have adopted a plan of reorganization first and then built appropriate schools.

97

But the need for rapid building militated against long-term planning. The Gateshead authority's problems stem not from its failures, but from its earlier successes.

The most striking thing about the interest groups in the story is how few of them there were. Groups such as industry, commerce, the churches (other than the Roman Catholics) and the trade unions, which might well have felt entitled to a say in the reshaping of secondary education, were conspicuous by their silence. In practice, only Old Students' associations, teachers' organizations, and the Roman Catholic Church call for consideration. The two former were active but not strikingly effective. The latter was passive and achieved virtually all it could have wished. The machinery of consultation seems, in both towns, to have been valuable as a pill-sweetener. But it is hard to detect any point where the plans finally adopted were modified by the advice given. Darlington N.U.T. believe that their pressure was effective in securing an increase in the size of the proposed schools. But the prediction of population growth in the Hailsham Plan seems to have counted for more.

Parents played some part in Darlington, especially since it may be assumed that the great majority of the 2,500 objectors to the Darlington 1958 scheme were moved by parental impulses. But in Gateshead their contribution was virtually nil. A correspondent from Canada wrote to the local Press that she was 'appalled ... that not one person wrote to you from the parents' point of view' (*Gateshead Post*, 16 April, 1966). Such an attitude recalls a passage from Conan Doyle's story 'Silver Blaze':

> ' "Is there any other point to which you would wish to draw my attention?"
> "To the curious incident of the dog in the night-time."
> "The dog did nothing in the night-time."
> "That was the curious incident," remarked Sherlock Holmes.'

Suggestions for further reading

There are few studies of the inner working of local authorities in general, and of educational policy-making in particular. The following short list of books simply indicates a selection of the relevant literature, without attempting to provide a complete bibliography.

G. BARON (1965), *Society, Schools & Progress in England*, Pergamon.

J. G. BULPITT (1967), *Party Politics in English Local Government*, Longmans.

T. BURGESS (1964), *Guide to English Schools*, Penguin.

J. A. G. GRIFFITH (1966), *Central Departments and Local Authorities*, Allen & Unwin.

R. M. JACKSON (2nd ed, 1965) *Machinery of Local Government*, Macmillan.

C. A. MOSER and W. SCOTT (1961), *British Towns*, Oliver & Boyd.

R. PEDLEY (1963), *The Comprehensive School*, Penguin.

D. PESCHEK and J. BRAND (1966), *Policies and Politics in Secondary Education*, Greater London Group.

M. M. WELLS and P. S. TAYLOR (5th ed, 1961), *New Law of Education*, Butterworth.

H. V. WISEMAN (1967), *Local Government at Work: a case study of a county borough*, Routledge & Kegan Paul.